D0290525

THE

CUSTOMER SERVICE SOLUTION

THE
CUSTOMER
SERVICE
SOLUTION

MANAGING EMOTIONS, TRUST, AND CONTROL TO
WIN YOUR CUSTOMER'S BUSINESS

Sriram Dasu, PhD and Richard B. Chase, PhD

New York   Chicago   San Francisco   Athens   London
Madrid   Mexico City   Milan   New Delhi
Singapore   Sydney   Toronto

Copyright © 2013 by Sriram Dasu and Richard B. Chase. All rights reserved. Printed in the United States of America. Except as permitted under the United States Copyright Act of 1976, no part of this publication may be reproduced or distributed in any form or by any means, or stored in a database or retrieval system, without the prior written permission of the publisher.

1 2 3 4 5 6 7 8 9 0   QFR/QFR   1 9 8 7 6 5 4 3

ISBN   978-0-07-180993-1
MHID   0-07-180993-7

e-ISBN   978-0-07-180999-3
e-MHID   0-07-180999-6

Library of Congress Cataloging-in-Publication Data
Dasu, Sriram.
  The customer service solution : managing emotions, trust, and control to win your customer's business / by Sriram Dasu and Richard Chase.
    pages cm
  ISBN 978-0-07-180993-1 (alk. paper) — ISBN 0-07-180993-7 (alk. paper)
    1. Customer relations. 2. Customer services. 3. Service industries—Management. I. Chase, Richard B. II. Title.
  HF5415.5.D175 2013
  658.8'12—dc23

                                                         2013006925

McGraw-Hill Education books are available at special quantity discounts to use as premiums and sales promotions or for use in corporate training programs. To contact a representative, please visit the Contact Us pages at www.mhprofessional.com.

This book is printed on acid-free paper.

To Rama and Harri

CONTENTS

TIME WARP: DURATION MANAGEMENT   139

ATTRIBUTION: ENSURING THAT YOU
GET YOUR DUE   169

PREFACE

We wrote this book because we believe that many companies are leaving some valuable service improvements on the table. These improvements derive from a deeper understanding and application of the psychology that underlies how customers "experience the service experience." We propose a collection of approaches for designing systems that deliver experiences. This book is about design and management of service operations.

In writing the book, we cherry-picked experimental research findings of the great minds in behavioral sciences and economics—D. Kahneman, G. F. Lowenstein, E. A. Skinner, V. Folkes, D. Ariely, J. Ledoux, C. E. Izard, D. Gambetta, and R. Larson—and translated them into service principles. We have also interviewed numerous executives and consultants from diverse companies and industries to get examples and share ideas about further application of our ideas in their companies.

The seminal book *The Experience Economy* by Pine and Gilmore ignited a lot of interest in customer experiences. The premise of the experience economy is that customers buy experiences and are willing to pay a steep premium for them, so managers should try to make these experiences more fun. Our book proposes how service operations can be redesigned using psychological principles to deliver good experiences on a consistent basis. Our concepts and methodology can be applied to any type of service, even services that do not readily lend themselves to theatrical experience concepts—that is, most everyday businesses. These may be primarily hedonic, like rock concerts and tourism, or largely utilitarian, like retirement planning and care for the chronically ill. As a result, the findings in this book are applicable to many different industries, including healthcare, hospitality, financial services, sports, and e-commerce.

We also believe that our solution addresses the major weakness inherent in service quality improvements from the old total quality management (TQM) to new Six Sigma programs—the lack of the psychological tools and concepts necessary for managers to create optimal service experiences. There are several reasons why existing quality approaches fall short. First, they are far more focused on the employee than on the customer; yes, a motivated, trained employee can do much to improve service, but he or she is limited by focusing on explicit customer expectations, not on implicit customer needs. (We have a lot more to say about this throughout the book.) Second, they are often bureaucratic exercises involving more statistics and scorekeeping than explaining how customers experience services at a subconscious level.

Another part of the problem that is endemic to the service industry, and we find in academia as well, is that the two disciplines that traditionally deal with managing customers in service organizations—operations management and marketing—haven't really gotten on the same page about customer experience management. Marketing people "know" the concepts we are presenting in the book but have never tried to make them readily applicable to real-world service design and operations management.

It is probably safe to say that we are the first operations management specialists to write such a book. Operations management (OM) is above all an applied field. While it draws upon various disciplines and theories, OM is essentially the design and operation of productive processes, be they manufacturing or service. Its prescriptions must be actionable in the real world: "The proof of the pudding is in the eating" pretty well sums up the practical nature of the field and the goal of this book. Bon appetit!

ACKNOWLEDGMENTS

We owe a major debt of gratitude to researchers in the behavioral science disciplines of economics, psychology, and sociology. Most notable among these is Nobel Prize winner Daniel Kahneman whose studies of how individuals process information at the subconscious level opened up a whole new way for us to think about service design.

We are deeply indebted to the following executives who were kind enough to let us interview them about service management in their organizations: Paul Allman, personnel training consultant; Odmar Almeida; Agatha Areas, Rock in Rio; Dr. Michele Burnison, Cedars Sinai; Gamal Aziz and Corrine Clement, MGM Hospitality; Krishna Ganugapati; Derrick Hall and Josh Rawitch, Arizona Diamondbacks; Stefan Isser, Swarovski; Ali Kasikci, Orient Express; Tony Knopp, Spotlight Ticket Management; Gary Loveman, Caesars Entertainment Group; Chris McGowan, A.E.G. Sports; Marc Mancini, Mancini Seminars and Consulting; Dr. Mildred Nelson, Christie Clinic; John Severini, California Restaurant Association; Rawn Shaw and James Spohrer, IBM; Mike Simms, Simms Restaurant Group; Dr. Chris Ullman; Becky Uzemeck; Lynne Walker and Shahid Moghul, Dell; and Pete Winemiller, Oklahoma Thunder.

We would like to thank our colleagues who have stimulated our thinking in various aspects of service over the years: James Heskett, Earl Sasser, and Frances Frei of Harvard University; Chris Voss of the London Business School; Uday Karmarker and Reza Ahmadi of UCLA; Richard Larson and Gabriel Bitran of MIT; Aleda Roth of Clemson University; Alexandra Brunner-Sperdin of the University of Innsbruck; Scott Sampson of Brigham Young University;

Cheryl Kimes and Rohit Verma of Cornell University; William Youngdahl of Arizona State University–West; David Bowen of the Thunderbird School of International Business; Lawrence Chase of California State University–Sacramento; Douglas Stewart of the University of New Mexico; Andreas Soteriou of Cyprus University; Deborah Kellogg of the University of Colorado–Denver; Mary Jo Bitner of Arizona State University; Thomas Roemer of UCSD; Paul Maglio of UC Merced; Mark Davis of Bentley; and our USC colleagues Yehuda Bassok, David Carter, Omar El Sawy, Valerie Folkes, Ravi Kumar, Deborah MacInnis, Raj Rajagopalan, and Jon Yormark.

Finally, we would like to thank Kellen Diamanti for her wonderful contributions to both the form and the content of the book; our McGraw-Hill Education team, including editors Mary Glenn and Thomas Miller, for their enthusiastic support throughout the publication process and editing manager Jane Palmieri; and our agent Jeffrey Krames, who helped shape our book proposal.

CUSTOMER SERVICE SOLUTIONS

LEVERAGING CUSTOMER PSYCHOLOGY TO DESIGN SERVICE OPERATIONS

> I know what I have given you. I do not know what you have received.
>
> —Antonio Porchia, Voces

Many service firms advocate the mantra TLC—think like a customer—in designing their service interactions. The problem is that they don't have a good handle on how customers really do think and as a result miss opportunities to become truly excellent. Indeed, while most successful service companies address the obvious things that affect customers' psychological attitude toward the service, such as courtesy and responsiveness on the part of their employees, they could do much more if they understood customer psychology at a deeper level.

The developed world's economies are dominated by service firms. This has come about not because of their excellence, but rather through a combination of market demand and creative development of new services. While the technologies that underlie service have evolved at a rapid rate, the approaches to designing and managing how the customer *experiences* the everyday delivery of service remain almost primitive.

Typical approaches to improving the service experience include analyzing customer satisfaction surveys, engaging in mystery shopping, and conducting focus group feedback sessions. These are all good, of course, but unfortunately customers cannot always articulate what shapes their perceptions and judgments, nor can company experts read between the lines to find out what drives customers. The result is often disappointing levels of customer satisfaction in general, even for companies that by all the standard criteria seem to be doing things right.

IMPLICIT OUTCOMES ARE IMPORTANT FOR YOUR CUSTOMERS

The first step in raising customer experience levels is recognizing the importance of implicit outcomes from a service encounter. The focus of service organizations is often on *explicit outcomes*, such as on-time flight arrivals or the time to resolve a customer's call. However, *subjective* or *implicit outcomes*, like emotions and feelings generated by a service encounter, are rarely considered. Did the passenger walk out of the airport *happy*? Did the customer *trust* the advice received by the service agent? Does the patient feel *motivated* enough to comply with the doctor's recommendation? At the end of the baseball season, is the fan sufficiently *excited* to renew her season tickets? When an accident victim calls his automobile insurance agent, does he feel more in *control* of his life?

A common assumption is that as long as the explicit outcomes are well managed, the customer experience will be great. Consider the following examples:

- Think about two rounds of golf in which your overall score is par. In one round on the eighteenth hole you shoot a double bogey, and in the other round you shoot a birdie. The outcome was the same, but wouldn't how you feel at the end, what you would recall about each experience, and how you summarize these experiences be very different?

- Jim and Mary are two longtime customers of a catalog retailer. The last purchase made by Jim was a bad experience, while Mary's was unremarkable. The next time Jim and Mary call the retailer, would they be paying attention to the same elements of the conversation?

At the core of our idea is that similar service encounters with identical explicit outcomes can be perceived very differently.

TYPES OF KNOWLEDGE NEEDED FOR DELIVERING IMPLICIT OUTCOMES

Explanations abound for why the delivery of service has not really moved beyond explicit outcomes. The most common explanation is that service encounters are intangible and that people-intensive processes are inherently unpredictable and hence uncontrollable. Thus by extension they are "undesignable." This view has been accepted and abetted by management books and articles that discuss service management as an art. Our current system of service delivery also has been allowed to prevail because a few exemplars have excelled at creating positive service cultures: friendliness and helpfulness at Apple Stores, the "everybody is a cast member" joyfulness of Disneyland, and the "ladies and gentlemen serve ladies and gentlemen" decorum of Ritz Carlton.

We hasten to point out that this cultural imprinting is no mean feat. Rather it is the bedrock of any effective service business. Unfortunately, most service executives don't recognize that what has been seen up to this point as the entire service experience is merely the platform, the necessary context for handling behavioral aspects of service. Getting to the next level calls for an understanding of service interactions that matches in depth and rigor the underlying goods production, or in the service sector, something akin to a medical procedure.

Carefully reengineering processes using techniques such as Six Sigma and lean enables firms to improve explicit outcomes and reduce costs. In other words, firms can achieve better quality at a lower cost. Those of us who have been in the quality business for many years no doubt recall the phrase "quality is free." Just as deeper understanding of systems dynamics and process analysis forms the bedrock of traditional process engineering techniques, findings from behavioral decision making, cognitive psychology, and social psychology can point service providers to ideas for redesigning the psychological or implicit aspects of service encounters.

Fortunately, we don't have to start from scratch. We have a virtual treasure trove of behavioral research findings. In this book we take these findings and for the first time discuss how firms can apply them *systematically* to the design and management of service processes.

The flavor of what we are talking about is captured in the following example. Danielle, a pediatric dental hygienist, has almost finished cleaning Spencer's teeth. Spencer is a skittish six-year-old who suffers from a mild form of gingivitis and has several cavities.

He is a frequent visitor to the clinic. Danielle suddenly finds that she has scraped a particularly sensitive spot. She still needs to clean two more teeth, which she is sure are not as sensitive. She could either terminate the procedure and resume on the next visit or complete the cleaning today. If she were to continue, she would subject Spencer to more discomfort, although significantly less than what just transpired.

In addition to medical concerns, there are other factors Danielle must consider in making her decision. How will this decision influence Spencer's perception of the cleaning experience and his behavior on subsequent visits? Wouldn't continuing increase the total pain and therefore render the experience even more unpleasant?

Findings in behavioral research suggest that continuing the procedure at lower levels of pain may actually cause people to have a less negative recall of the experience. In this case, Spencer would remember the little incident, of course, but also that the pain "wasn't so bad at the end." If Danielle applies these counterintuitive findings in behavioral science to shape the service encounter—lengthen the experience and end with less pain—she will improve Spencer's perception of the appointment.

This brings us to the issue of why understanding customer psychology helps managers deliver better service. First it helps them understand what shapes customers' perceptions and how customers summarize and recall experiences. As we see in the example above, customers employ heuristics and rules that they cannot always articulate. Second, in other cases the feelings and emotions that drive a customer's perceptions might be obvious if the firm had processes in place to detect them. Take for instance the example of Jim and Mary, who had different prior experiences with a catalog retailer. If the customer representatives were aware of the caller's history, they could adapt their responses accordingly. This could make a difference to Jim in particular because his previous call did not go well. Even the customer service agent will benefit if he or she knew before answering the call that Jim may be angry or annoyed. The third reason is that managing service interactions can be very complex because of the large number of employees involved in delivering a service or because there are seemingly too many factors that may shape the implicit outputs. MGM Grand and Farmers Insurance each employs tens of thousands of employees, and these employees interact with millions of customers in a wide variety of situations. In other settings, such as healthcare, the customer often enters the system highly flustered with a complex set of emotions. The employees are trained to focus on taking care of the explicit concerns, in this case health-related issues, and may not have the skills, knowledge, or motivation to address the implicit concerns, such as the anxiety and stress of the customer.

The purpose of this book is to identify the rules that customers employ to summarize experiences—the factors that shape their perceptions—and present methods for systematically designing service processes to deliver implicit outcomes. We accomplish this by leveraging findings in social sciences, cognitive sciences, and behavioral decision making.

PARSING THE SERVICE ENCOUNTER

A service encounter consists of a customer interacting with an organization for the purpose of achieving some goal. The interaction may be either face-to-face or through telecommunications. It could be a single interaction, such as buying an airline ticket, or one of a series of interactions that is required to complete the service, such as airline check-in, flying, retrieving luggage, and so on. Encounters also occur over extended periods of time, such as multiple visits with a real estate agent when people are buying a new home or meetings with an obstetrician during various stages of a woman's pregnancy.

The issue is how to improve such encounters. A major inhibitor to achieving this goal is the lack of precision in scientifically defining the fundamental elements that take place during the encounter. The problem lies in the word *service* itself. It is a blanket term that means different things to different people. If we say we had great service at a bank, it doesn't tell us what was great about it. Usually it is a combination of things working well together, but without further analysis, the term *service* fails to make the important distinction between the work required to provide the service and the attitudes of service personnel who deliver it. To address this problem, as well as others surrounding services, we need to do what every other science does: establish operational definitions that permit focused analysis of cause and effect. A useful such categorization is the three Ts (see box).

An encounter can be operationally defined as consisting of three Ts: the task to be done, the treatment accorded the customer, and the tangible (and sensory) features of the service. Thus when getting a car serviced, for example, we can ask whether the work was performed satisfactorily and completed on time (task). Was the server friendly (treatment)? And was the waiting room clean and pleasant (tangible)? Of course we can go into more depth with each of these, depending upon what level of detail we are after.

IT IS ALL ABOUT YOUR CUSTOMERS' PERCEPTIONS

Ultimately what matters is how customers perceive a service encounter. Each service consists of a core task. How this task is executed shapes our perceptions of the encounter. We want to reemphasize that the core task can almost always be accomplished in multiple ways and that the perceived experience can be very different from customer to customer. In the foregoing example, Danielle could have achieved the same medical outcome in a number of ways. She could have, for example, deferred the most painful part of the procedure to the end, assuming that she could let the child go immediately after. But whatever her choice, it would have had considerable bearing on little Spencer's perceptions of the experience. Even though it doesn't seem like extending pain would be *better* for the customer, this is just another nonintuitive rule for summarizing experiences.

Obviously positive recollections of past experiences encourage customers to come back. Therefore, the more managers understand the science behind how we evaluate experiences, why we attribute blame or credit, and how memories are created and recalled, the better they know what constitutes a positive experience and the more effective a job they can do in the design and management of service encounters. In the design area, for example, such knowledge is useful for planning the number of stages of the service, the sequence in which events occur, the duration of the events, the frequency of "touching" customers as service unfolds, the types of information shared, the nature of the interpersonal interaction, the layout of service facilities, and the technology requirements. In the management area, this knowledge, coupled with behavioral findings on communication and culture, can help managers with staff selection and training.

FACTORS THAT SHAPE YOUR CUSTOMERS' PERCEPTIONS

We have identified six closely interrelated factors that shape perceptions. The first is the sequence in which the events unfold; the second is the duration of different events and our perception of time; and the third is the degree of control and choice given to the customer. These first three factors can be directly incorporated into the design of the service system. These influence the next three factors, trust, emotions, and the attribution of blame or credit for a bad or good experience (see Figure 1.1).

Often the customer and server have to work together to create the output. What each player observes and how he or she reacts and

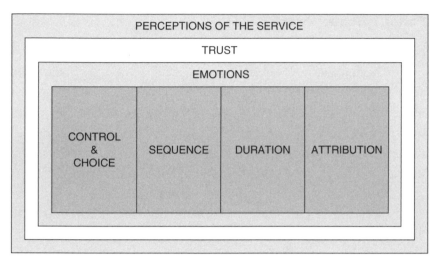

Figure 1.1 Six elements of service

cooperates depend on the degree of trust they have in each other and on their emotional states. The outcome of each event in turn influences trust and emotions. These two factors can be thought of as platforms on which the service encounter takes place.

Once the service is completed, customers attribute success or failure. The final factor we explore is the heuristics used by consumers to lay blame or give credit.

The ETCs of Service

Throughout the book we use the abbreviation ETCs when referring to the general set of psychological concepts we are presenting. The ETCs—Emotions, Trust, Control, and sequence—were the centerpieces of our earlier work. In thinking about service design, it seemed clear that, far from being just incidental elements in a service as the term "etc." implies, they, along with duration and attribution, may well be the difference makers in service excellence.

Factor 1: Sequence of Events

All service experiences consist of series of events that occur over time. The tendency of laypeople is to focus on a strong start and assume that things will subsequently take care of themselves. At the other extreme we have service folklore that suggests that every minute is significant. Neither belief is accurate. In fact, a few pivotal moments have a disproportionately large bearing on how we summarize and recall an experience; one of those pivotal moments, as we have seen above, is the end of the transaction.

To illustrate this idea, consider a 7-hour drive from San Francisco to Los Angeles, during which the first 45 minutes are in stop-and-go traffic and the rest of the journey is at the speed limit. Compare this to another 7-hour journey between the same cities, during which only the last 45 minutes are in stop-and-go traffic. Are the two journeys perceived the same way? The person hitting traffic at the end of the journey will likely have stronger memories of the negatives of the trip, while the person who got the pain out of the way first will come away with stronger feelings that the overall trip went well because it ended well.

Does this mean the start does not matter? Take, for example, a third 7-hour trip from San Francisco to Los Angeles that begins with 25 minutes of bad traffic, the middle of the journey at the speed limit, and the last 20 minutes of bad traffic again. The initial 25 minutes set the precedent for the traveler to possibly add stronger negative feelings to the traffic at the end of the trip.

The main point is that the sequence in which events unfold and the key moments such as highs, lows, and endings have a bearing on how we perceive an experience. We find that managers rarely pay attention to the sequence effects, in particular the role of the ending. In the chapter on sequence effects, we delve into the following questions:

- How can firms alter the sequence of events to improve perceptions of an experience?

- Does the sequence effect apply to all types of services, including grocery stores, retail banking, rock concerts, and obstetrics? Or is it only limited to some types of services?

- How important is a peak event? Should firms ensure that all moments are equally good, or is it optimal to invest in a unique highlight?

Factor 2: Duration of Experiences

Time is an integral part of any service, and service managers do worry about duration. Much of traditional process improvement efforts are directed at reducing processing and waiting times. Nevertheless, waiting is unavoidable. Not every chore can be done instantly, and all good things do come to an end. This brings us to perception of time. To illustrate the psychology of time, consider two situations. In the first, you wait 20 minutes for a radiology report, and then have to wait another 20 minutes for a blood analysis report. So you experience a combined wait of 40 minutes for both reports. The two situations would likely generate different levels of dissatisfaction. Further, how would your perception of time be affected if patients who arrived after you were served before you?

We all know that an hour is not an hour. How quickly it passes depends on a number of factors, such as whether we are involved in pleasant or unpleasant activities, whether we are paying attention to the passage of time, how many segments the experience is divided into, and so on. Therefore,

- How can firms make positive events seem longer and negative events seem shorter?

- Is it possible for waiting to improve the service experience? Is there value in building anticipation? When should firms build anticipation? How can firms build anticipation?

Factor 3: Control and Choice

Our ability to control our lives is vital to our mental health. After all, imprisonment is the highest form of punishment and minimizes the control a criminal has over his or her life. As a thought exercise, imagine that you are flying from Los Angeles to Munich in a middle economy seat between two strangers. You may experience a feeling of loss of control, partly because you don't know how the experience will evolve. A range of life events, both positive and negative, leave us bewildered. These events include car accidents, developing a chronic disease, getting a big unexpected promotion, discovering that your risky investment has grown thirtyfold, and expecting a baby. Indeed, the greater the personal risk or investment in time or money, the greater the need for perceived control.

In virtually every service encounter, customers must relinquish some actual control to the service firm in order to get the job done. Yet we as customers prefer situations in which we perceive that we have control.

We perceive control when two conditions exist. The first is choice, such as when we are able to select from various components necessary for the desired service, like being able to select which hairstylist to use at a salon. The second is capacity. In this situation, we have the ability to influence the behavior of the service provider in order for us to achieve our objectives, such as having the hairstylist cut our hair the way we want it cut.

Research in many service settings has shown that there is a relationship between perceptions of control and levels of satisfaction. For example, studies in healthcare management have consistently shown that when patients have reasonable control over their treatment regimens, they are more satisfied than when doctors are in total control. Even simple options, such as allowing a patient to choose from which arm to draw blood, result in the patient feeling less pain than when the patient is not given a choice.

Perceived control is affected not only by the decisions that are delegated to the customer but also by such factors as the perceived complexity of the technology used in the encounter and the size of the crowd at the service setting. Regarding technology, some senior citizens, for example, fear loss of control in dealing with bank ATMs and prefer to wait in line to hand their money to a teller. One way to deal with this problem is the "back to the future" approach used by First Republic Bank in San Francisco. This bank encourages its customers to come to the branch and have the teller handle the transaction.

Regarding crowding, many of us feel a loss of control in crowds. Here the question is at what point does the neutral perception of crowd density become the unpleasant perception of crowding? One of the ways that has been found to reduce the negative effects of crowding is to increase cognitive control by informing people about the likely effects of crowding before they are immersed in a crowd. An example would be a loudspeaker announcement informing riders on the subway that the dispatcher has added extra cars to handle a large crowd after a sporting event. Those stuck in the subway with the crowd feel a greater sense of control simply by being armed with the knowledge that something is being done about the situation.

Important issues concerning control and choice include:

- How can firms frame service encounters to maximize the customer's perception of control?

- Where should firms introduce control choices to an encounter?

- Offering greater choice has resource implications for the firm and may place greater demands on consumers' decision processes. Which decisions should the customer control and which should the firm control?

Factor 4: Emotions

Our perceptions of events are almost always affected by the emotions we bring to the situation and the emotions generated by an encounter. People who are upset or nervous prior to an encounter will be more difficult to serve than those who are calm at the outset. In the case of Spencer, for example, there are actions the dentist can take, such as having a fun waiting room and soothing or fun distractions for children before they undergo the teeth cleaning. Spencer's time in the waiting room would raise his positive emotional state prior to the cleaning, making him easier to serve, and therefore bring about a more positive service experience.

One of the emotions sought in many service encounters is that of delight. This has received considerable attention lately among so-called experience economy companies that talk about converting everyday services to memorable experiences that "delight the customer." However, lost in the rush to apply concepts employed by Disney, such as adding play and entertainment to malls and banks, is the need to understand that delight can be experienced in different ways. Managers associate delight with exceeding expectations, which is not necessarily true. Sometimes delight comes from surprise, such as, "You won our drawing for X," but other times it comes from creating a predictable, pleasant experience that develops into an enduring and endearing relationship with the company. For example, knowing that your Double-Double burger and fries at In-N-Out Burger are freshly prepared before your eyes and taste how they should create a delight emotion that makes you a return customer. There are many experiences and services that we repeatedly consume because they are delightfully predictable.

Focusing solely on delight has several significant limitations. For one, delight as it is understood in service folklore is too broad a concept and ignores other positive emotions. The thrill of being on a roller coaster in Magic Mountain differs from the feeling of becoming a parent for the first time, and this in turn differs from the feelings of a saleswoman who completes the sale of a large order to an important customer. These events differ in terms of who is responsible for the positive outcome and therefore in the type of emotion generated. The positive emotions you want to accentuate in a management consulting encounter are different from those you want people to experience at a Marriott resort.

Furthermore, for service managers the service encounter is not always about positive emotions. Service providers frequently have to deal with negative emotions ranging from anxiety to anger. How do we convey negative information? For example, bad weather like a hurricane in the gulf might mean the grounding of flights as well as the delay of trains and trucks, which in turn means the delay in shipments of goods. How should a salesperson handle the possibility of a delay in delivering an important order? Does framing and timing of the information change whom the buyer holds accountable for the delay? Does attribution in turn change the types of emotions generated?

There are also practical challenges for anticipating emotions. Alpert, a friend's eight-year-old son, slipped and fell while running at the zoo and had to be taken to the emergency room. Alpert's mother, Liz, went with Alpert in the ambulance, while her friend Martha took care of Alpert's younger sister along with her own two children. The zoo manager escorted Martha and the children to her car, provided her with directions to the hospital, and was very considerate. Most of us would be appreciative of the zoo manager's attention, and at the same time we would believe that the manager's response was obviously the right thing to do given the anxiety and stress of the visitors.

Now let us consider another of Martha's experiences. Martha had a minor surgical procedure on her hand. Her insurance policy allowed her considerable latitude in selecting surgeons from a preferred provider network and those outside the network. Several months after the surgery was over she received a $2,000 check from the insurance company to pay for the cost of the surgery and an $18,000 bill from the hospital. The bill came as a shock to Martha. When she called her health insurance company, the representative responded flatly that because the surgeon was not from the network, it was up to Martha to cover the amount. She suggested that Martha try negotiating with the hospital and that there was nothing the insurance company would do. As with the zoo experience, it is not difficult to predict Martha's emotions. Yet, Martha's experience with the service agent's complete lack of concern for how Martha might feel is all too familiar. These two stories illustrate one of the points of this book—that there is an opportunity for firms to systematically anticipate emotions and respond appropriately. This is one of the keys to delivering implicit outputs. In fairness to the insurance company, we want to note that the story had a happy ending. Martha called back the next day, and the new agent understood her predicament and guided her through the process. Martha did not incur any out-of-pocket expenses.

Creating a good experience requires an understanding of what triggers different types of positive and negative emotions. This allows managers at an aggregate level to develop what we call an emotional platform and at a tactical or process level to identify stages within the systems that are likely to engender strong emotions. Being aware of emotional triggers within the process creates an opportunity for managers to proactively manage emotions and thereby create an emotionally intelligent organization. For example, one of the problems with call centers is that scripting makes socioemotional interactions appear wooden or contrived. However, anticipating emotions based on the nature of the transaction enables the agent to respond with greater authenticity. In the chapter on emotions we address the following questions:

- How can firms anticipate emotions?

- How can firms proactively mitigate negative emotions and enhance positive emotions?

- Some firms use emotions to differentiate and brand a service. How can transactions be designed to be consistent with the overall brand image?

Factor 5: Trust

Trust is a critical factor in ensuring successful service encounters. We trust our bank to protect us from fraudulent usage of a debit card, and the investment analyst has a better understanding of the stock market than you do. Unlike other factors affecting perceptions, trust is shaped by an explicit contract made before the service is delivered. In services, caveat vendor applies as much as caveat emptor does. Both parties contribute toward the outcome, and things can go well or badly for both. Contracts are rarely complete, except perhaps in services that are predominantly transactional in nature. A study by McKinsey[1] found that the transactional component of work done in the United States is decreasing and that an increasingly large percent is tacit. Hence, trust is important because a contractual arrangement cannot ensure satisfactory performance. Given that both parties are vulnerable to the actions of the other, developing a sense of trust is crucial.

How do you develop trust? Consistently delivering positive outcomes will certainly engender a sense of trust. Unfortunately, except in the most basic services, this is not possible. Medical procedures, lawsuits, management consulting engagements, software development projects, and engineering projects frequently have ambiguous outcomes. There is almost always a lingering doubt about whether the results could have been better.

Most high value-added services involve knowledge workers. They are also characterized by asymmetric information and an inability to objectively judge the outcome. An example from the world of engineering services illustrates this point well. Biosense Webster, a subsidiary of Johnson & Johnson, contracted with a small machine tool manufacturer to supply a customized lathe. The manufacturer had to modify one of its products to meet Biosense Webster's requirements. After a year, the project was abandoned by mutual consent. The buyers felt that the supplier failed to meet the requirements. The supplier maintained that the buyer failed to clearly articulate the specifications in the first place.

Biosense Webster engineers entered into a contract without a complete understanding of the requirements, and they were dependent on the expertise of the engineers of the supplier to determine what was feasible. The contract was problematic because the firms had different knowledge sets. When the project outcome was not perfect, both parties shared some responsibility thus making it difficult to clearly assign blame or unambiguously evaluate competence. Will Biosense Webster go back to this supplier in the future? The answer depends on whether Biosense trusts the supplier to deliver on the next project.

To understand how trust is built, we need to understand different kinds of trust and how each kind is realized. There are differences between kinds of trust that exist between organizations, between individuals, and between individuals and organizations. Trust is necessary because of a combination of uncertainty, dependency, and lack of information. Because objective information about performance is not adequate, trust is also developed on the basis of emotional affinities. In other words, there is both a cognitive and an emotional aspect to trust.

At an aggregate level, building a strong brand conveys a sense of competence. There are also many opportunities at the service delivery level to develop trust. Returning to the Biosense example, the level of trust in the supplier would depend on whether there was evidence of competence and diligence. The key issues include:

- How do customers judge the competence and motivation of a service provider?

- What are the events that add or detract from a service provider's trustworthiness?

- How can firms signal their competence and motivation to act in the customer's best interest? In particular, how can a professional convey competence to a customer who may not have the capability to evaluate the server's expertise?

Factor 6: Attribution

The psychology of how individuals make connections between cause and effect is fascinating. For service design, attribution theory can provide insights into how people rationalize the outcome of an encounter. One such insight is that we are predisposed to accept responsibility for success and reject responsibility for failure. As professors, we see this after an exam: the student who got an A says it came from hitting the books, while the student who got a C complains that the questions were unfair. Businesspeople see this in just about every form of personnel evaluation.

A second insight from attribution theory is that we overestimate our ability to cause an outcome that is actually determined by chance. In general, we want an explanation for every outcome. Chance as an explanation just doesn't sit well with us. When things go wrong, we are uncomfortable that a confluence of minor events could have caused the undesirable outcome, and instead we look for a single cause. Often, this cause is seen as the last event that happened. For example, how often have we attributed an unanticipated extra half hour of shopping time at a market to the one minute of extra time spent at the checkout line, rather than to the crowded store or a forgotten shopping list?

A third insight from attribution theory is that we believe that our own behaviors are determined predominantly by situational factors whereas other people's behaviors are caused mainly by their personality traits. Back at the supermarket, if you loudly chide the clerk to speed up, it's because the situation calls for someone to "get things moving." If you are not in a hurry and some unsavory looking fellow makes the same comments, you think he's a jerk.

A good grasp of how we make attributions should help service providers carry the burden of no more than their share of blame and receive at least the credit that is due. More important, these insights can be used to avoid sticky situations in the first place:

- How can firms ensure that customers give credit to service providers who do a good job?

- How can firms minimize the long-term consequences of poor service?

A SCIENTIFIC APPROACH TO DELIVERING GREAT EXPERIENCES

Developments in the global economy make how the behavioral side of service encounters are handled highly relevant to any manager. Standing out among these developments is the deskilling of jobs resulting from automation and offshoring of service work. A prerequisite for automation and offshoring is an explicit, rather than tacit, understanding of the production formulas. We understand this extremely well in the traditional manufacturing world. Process improvement systems such as Six Sigma and lean are based on scientific principles and have been described as the application of science to everyday business. In this book we identify a collection of behavioral principles that can be used to systematically improve the soft side, psychological aspects, or implicit outputs of a service experience.

Consider the questions that must be addressed in determining how to deal with a customer with problems at a call center. What should the flow of the interaction be like? Should you give bad news at the start of the conversation or at the end? How should you frame a response or break a conversation when things appear to be going downhill? How can you give directions to callers without making them feel incompetent? How can you engender trust? What factors enhance the memory of the process to make the customers feel more open to the use of the call center? Each of these issues also involves the training of call center workers. Similar issues have to be addressed by Realtors, investment advisors, doctors, nurses, hoteliers, resort managers, managers of sporting events, and so on.

There are exciting developments in the behavioral sciences in such areas as memory, emotions, and behavioral decision theory. (For example, the work of Nobel Prize winning psychologist Daniel Kahneman bears directly on aspects of flow and sequencing of encounters.) There are recent studies that address how important emotional connections between the customer and the organization are to the success of an organization.[2]

BEYOND THE ENCOUNTER:
MEMORY MANAGEMENT

What a business ideally wishes to do is to see inside each customer's mind to see what memories already exist and to then tailor services to fit in with the positive ones. In fact, in many respects, the goal of service encounter designers is memory management. In this book, we focus on what happens during service encounters, but there is a need to go beyond the encounter.

Memory management must address two dimensions: a hedonic dimension that strives to maximize pleasant memories and minimize unpleasant ones, and an operational dimension that strives to facilitate the customer's activities in partaking of the service. Memory research has provided a number of insights that help us in both these dimensions.

One that is particularly pertinent for hedonic memories is that information acquired after an experience can transform the memory of that experience. In recall and recognition, people tend to include ideas or elements inferred or related to the original experience but that are not actually part of the original experience itself. Thus, in Spencer's case, his mother might convert the general negative hedonic recollection of the dentist visit by pointing out the fun that he experienced in the waiting area. (Of course, on subsequent visits, there had better be a fun component!)

Another is that our memories are modified by expectations of what should happen based upon the experiences of others. This is frequently seen in people's recollection of the quality of service they have received. A less-than-wonderful shopping experience at Nordstrom may be dissipated by the fact that "everybody praises the store for its service," and thus the shopper feels obliged to report a positive overall evaluation of the company.

One of the ways to enhance operational memory is through the use of the "overlap principle." The idea is that memory of what to do improves to the extent that the elements of the current environment overlap with the elements of the past events. That is, if you recall everything in the background (temperature, noise, people, layout, current emotional state, etc.) as the same as when the memory was first acquired, then recollection will be enhanced. The practical implication for services is, "Don't rearrange things too often." Make service interactions consistent. (Unless of course, the current process is broken, in which case you want to change the drill, scenery, etc.) Examples of businesses that successfully use the overlap principle include Starbucks, Olive Garden, and Ikea.

In short, developments in social science that we identify in this book provide managers with a tremendous opportunity to push their service experiences to the next level of excellence. The beauty of understanding how customers process experiences at a deeper level is that it enables firms to embed into their processes the ability to deliver certain psychological outcomes on a consistent basis. This approach to hard wiring the soft side of service design has the potential to decrease the burden of emotional labor. It also allows the firm to leverage the capability of emotionally intelligent employees. Finally as we discovered in the 1980s in the context of traditional process improvement, quality can be free. In our case, we contend that firms can offer superior experiences without incurring additional costs.

CHAPTER 2

DESIGNING EMOTIONALLY INTELLIGENT PROCESSES

People will forget what you said, people
will forget what you do, but people will
never forget how you made them feel.

—Jason Barger

You're planning a surprise anniversary trip to Hawaii, so you contact a resort to make reservations. A dull pain in your abdomen sends you to the nearest urgent care facility. Your teenage son lost his smartphone at the mall, so you call your cell phone provider. These are all goal-directed activities, and you're looking for specific outcomes. Each activity is also fraught with emotions, some negative (irritation, fear) and some positive (excitement, anticipation). For the service provider to create a memorable experience and to increase customer loyalty, which approach is likely to work best: ignore the emotions and focus on efficiently achieving the goals, or address the emotional aspects in addition to accomplishing the goals?

In the case of the missing smartphone, the customer support representative checks your son's phone logs while you wait on the line. Fortunately, the phone hasn't been used since the boy lost it. Following the first approach, the rep might say, "We have placed a lock on the phone." Following the second approach, the rep might say, "You don't need to worry about unauthorized use. We've placed a lock on the phone."

Certainly, both responses achieve the same objective; namely, you learn that a thief or opportunist cannot use the phone. Only the second response, however, acknowledges and addresses your anxiety. If this seems like unnecessary hand-holding, consider the role emotions actually play in shaping our perceptions, judgments, and memories.

EMOTIONS 101

Let's review the critical role emotions play in services.

Emotions Define the Importance of an Experience

Emotions, or feeling states, are fundamental parts of every experience. In *How the Mind Works*, psychologist Steven Pinker identifies emotions as "mechanisms that set the brain's highest-level goals." Their intensity indicates to us the immediate significance of a *particular* goal or outcome for an encounter. Pinker further points out that in many situations—such as choosing between two appealing movies—a purely rational machine would have no basis for selecting an action.

Emotions Shape Your Customers' Memories of Experiences

Emotions influence the mechanisms by which our brains store memories of events. We have an explicit, or conscious, memory that we use to access an event from the past. We also have an implicit, or unconscious, emotional memory that recalls the feelings we had during that event. Generally, emotionally charged events are the ones we recall most vividly. Neuroscientist Joseph LeDoux derived these principles in the course of his research on conditioned responses, during which he encountered the fascinating hat pin experiment.[1] It showed that we store emotional memories even when we can't access them consciously.

The Hat Pin Experiment

In 1911, Swiss physician Édouard Claparède reported on his work with a female patient suffering from anterograde amnesia. A localized brain injury had cost her all ability to form new memories, though long-term memories created prior to the injury remained intact. This meant that each time he encountered her, Claparède had to reintroduce himself, even if he had stepped away for only a moment. One day, Claparède hid a pin between his fingers and pricked the patient's hand when he shook it during his umpteenth formal introduction on entering. The experience, needless to say, was painful for the patient. The next time Claparède greeted her, she still didn't remember him and yet she refused to shake his hand although she couldn't explain why.

LeDoux cites the experiment to illustrate his deduction that we have both an "implicit emotional memory and an explicit memory of the emotional learning experience." He says that the normal, undamaged brain simultaneously forms an explicit memory and an implicit emotional memory of an event. The fearful response of Claparède's patient was based on her brain storing the emotional memory but not the conscious one.

People in service operations can learn important lessons by grasping the fact that customer interactions with service systems and service providers create emotional memories. As with Claparède's patient, feelings associated with the service encounter subsequently influence customers' recollections and attitudes toward the service provider. In addition, experiences that generate strong emotions are remembered for a long time. We cherish for a lifetime highly charged emotional events such as attending the Super Bowl, experiencing the birth of a child, visiting the Taj Mahal, or kayaking among dolphins near Captain Cook's monument in Hawaii. Remember that the same is true of traumatic events; we never forget them.

Emotions Influence Your Customers' Decisions

Until fairly recently, it was commonly accepted that emotions caused behavior. In recent years, however, evolutionary psychologists have been toying with the notion that we have it backwards. They're starting to see that emotions can also serve as feedback mechanisms stimulating us to think about and sometimes learn from the incident. Pinker calls them adaptive, based on eons of experience. One might legitimately describe emotions as a form of wisdom.

In our example of a lost smartphone, the feelings followed an event and, in turn, influenced the activity aimed at resolution. Regardless of how furious a father might be at his son's negligence, anger is not the deciding factor in his calling the cell phone company, but it may affect his interaction with the provider. So may other feelings such as patience or pessimism, which may arise from past dealings with support reps and inform the current interaction.

Even the fear arising from a never-before-felt pain in the chest can be regarded as the product of experience, whether from reading about heart disease, knowing someone who had a heart attack, or being warned by your doctor to lower your cholesterol.

Emotions Shape Your Customers' Responses

Service providers profit when the emotions that their customers and their employees experience put them in a positive frame of mind. In addition to creating positive memories, a number of other immediate benefits flow from prolonged upbeat feelings that turn into a good mood. Customers enjoying a good mood are more likely than those in a foul humor to remain onsite and tolerate business lapses, waits, and other inconveniences. They're more inclined to react charitably to minor substandard results, too, such as irregular packaging or a late delivery. On the other side of the service encounter, the company also benefits from employees who are in a good mood when they're working, because happy employees tend to be helpful to customers and company management. They are more likely to creatively solve problems than to impatiently watch the clock. All told, customers and employees who interact while they're in a good mood greatly increase the chances of duplicating desirable behaviors; they are likely to follow instructions, evaluate situations, and wait for outcomes.

Emotions Are the Outcomes of the Experience

Although satisfaction is frequently the lone criterion applied to managerial decision making and operations, it typically fails to capture the essence of the customer experience. When you ask people how their vacation or visit to an amusement park went, they are not likely to sum up the experience in terms of being satisfied or dissatisfied. When gamblers go to Las Vegas, they aren't seeking satisfaction, either. They want the thrill and excitement of hitting the jackpot.

Now imagine that your new wide-screen, high-definition television is delivered just in time for the Super Bowl, and it doesn't work. The retailer, moreover, informs you that it will not replace the set and that you need to contact the manufacturer. It's a safe bet that *dissatisfied* doesn't even come close to capturing your reaction. Like returning vacationers, we are likely to describe service experiences—good or bad—in emotional terms.

Service marketers otherwise content with the criterion of satisfaction are known to chase delight as the one emotion thought to elicit customer loyalty. Although delight is an emotional state, customers aren't known to describe their feeling as one of delight, even when the service experience is very positive. They're more likely to say that they are happy, thrilled, or excited.

Emotions Drive Your Customers' Loyalty

Customer loyalty, as indicated by repeat business and favorable word-of-mouth, is the clearest sign that a customer likes the company and the service provided. Besides any rational assessment of task performance, a positive emotional response drives loyalty. A case in point is a study that found that "the emotions a guest feels during a hotel stay are a critical component of satisfaction and loyalty."[2] In fact, customers who expressed positive emotional reactions to a hotel were also willing to pay a higher price for higher service levels. On a broad range of customer-provider relations, emotions such as frustration, anger, disappointment, anxiety, joy, happiness, hope, relief, and excitement exert a significant impact on behaviors that denote the presence or absence of customer loyalty, including repeat business, word-of-mouth referrals, and complaints. Finally, firms that generate feelings of pride and confidence are most likely to have loyal customers.

Brands and Emotions Are Linked

Brands play an important role in consumer choice and loyalty because they signal quality and summarize perceptions about the company that owns the brand.[3] Brand equity, or the value of having a well-known brand, depends on the customer connection to it, and this depends on functional aspects of the service and on intangibles such as the brand personality.[4] And wrapped up in the brand's personality are the various emotions that it evokes. In the service sector, many firms explicitly communicate the feelings or emotions they want customers to associate with their brand. Examples abound, illustrating the importance of emotions in positioning and differentiating service firms:

- Kaiser Permanente, a managed care consortium, exhorts its customers to "thrive," using ads that focus on ways to live healthier lives.

- The Tyrolean Tourism Board markets ski resorts in the Austrian Tyrol using the tag line "so nah, so fern" ("so near, so far") to tell people that they don't have to go far to feel like they've truly escaped.

- Virgin Airlines encourages us to "travel the world the Virgin way," inviting customers to discover its distinctive and rather "jet-setty" approach to air travel with its witty safety videos, touch-screen food and drink ordering, and Wi-Fi access.

- Zappos, the online shoe retailer, guarantees free shipping and free returns and uses puns and popular cultural references to project a fun shopping experience, like, "You're gonna need a bigger shoe rack. Way bigger" (*Jaws*), "Best in Snow" (*Best in Show*), and "Reclaim your side of the closet" (for menswear).

SERVICES DIFFER IN THEIR EMOTIONAL CONTENT

Thus far we have argued for the importance of emotions in a service encounter, but you may question the implication that all transactions are infused with emotion. Think about it. That coffee you drink in the morning wakes you up, but you may also find yourself feeling a bit of a glow. Most goods and services combine *utilitarian* and *hedonic* elements. Purely utilitarian services such as postal services, utilities, or gas stations are likely to contain minimal emotional content. Nevertheless, dry cleaning services, primarily a utilitarian chore, may evoke a very personal set of feelings: for some it is tedium and dislike, while others may enjoy a mild sense of accomplishment. At the other extreme, we have purely hedonic services that are heavily weighted with emotion, such as zip-lining in the Costa Rican rain forest, surfing at Waikiki, playing blackjack at the MGM Grand, or attending an opera at Teatro Colón in Buenos Aires. The main goal of services such as these is exhilaration, fun, or aesthetic stimulation, and they combine escapism with other hedonic components that are very real. For instance, when you attend an NBA game, the game itself is an escape, but the comfort of the seats is real, if, in fact, the seats are comfortable.

Regardless of whether a service is primarily utilitarian or primarily hedonic, the desire to generate or avoid a set of feelings influences our service consumption decisions. Figure 2.1 classifies services based on their hedonic content and associates them with either positive or negative feelings.

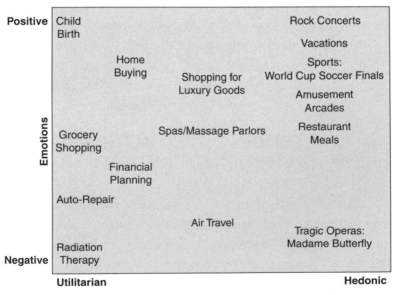

Figure 2.1 Hedonic and utilitarian nature of different services

EMOTIONS AND EMOTIONAL INTELLIGENCE

Because emotions are a universal part of services, providers need to ensure that the service delivery occurs in an emotionally "intelligent" manner. *Emotional intelligence* is the ability to perceive, evaluate, and control emotions. An organizational culture oriented to the customer is vital, but it isn't enough to ensure that service is delivered with emotional intelligence. Furthermore, while emotionally intelligent servers are valuable assets, they are often in short supply. And service providers fear that they're shouldering an excessive burden by taking on emotional work.[5]

One possibility for marrying service and emotional intelligence is to embed a certain amount of emotional intelligence into the mechanics of the delivery system. Building it directly into the system reduces the personal burden of emotional labor and better leverages intrinsically emotionally intelligent employees. Also, as transactions migrate to the Internet, we have no choice but to develop emotionally intelligent systems or give up on customer service. In the following, we delve a little deeper into theories about emotions in order to identify strategies for accentuating positive emotions and mitigating negative emotions in service encounters.

FACTORS THAT DRIVE YOUR CUSTOMERS' EMOTIONS

Superficially, the term "emotion" is easy to understand, but precisely defining and measuring individual emotions have been major challenges for the scientific community, resulting in many systems of classification. Robert Plutchik's well-known psychoevolutionary theory of emotion recognizes eight primary emotions—joy, sadness, anger, fear, disgust, anticipation, trust, and surprise—which can be combined and weighted to describe the full complement of human experience.[6] These basic emotions are common across all human cultures. Some are also displayed by other species. Sports fans grin and whoop for joy when their team scores the winning point, and they grimace and roar with frustration if the ref negates the score. Primates and dogs have similar reactions. Generally speaking, emotions are either pleasant or unpleasant, joy being pleasant, and anger being unpleasant. And, of course, an intense shift in emotion renders us susceptible to an altered mood.

One of the most compelling ways to classify emotions from an operational perspective uses appraisal theory, which specifies the conditions that produce different emotions. Appraisal theory identifies five factors that cause us to experience emotions singly or in combination. The feeling we experience depends on whether the:

- Change in outcome improves our situation or makes it worse

- Outcome is associated with a penalty or a reward

- Outcome is certain or just a possibility

- Causal event is significant or powerful and its resultant change easy to cope with, difficult to cope with, or insignificant

- Responsibility for the event and incumbent change falls on us or on an outside agency

We become emotional as soon as we encounter a change in outcomes, both potential and real. We experience fear and anger when the truck ahead of us on the highway suddenly swerves into our lane. We feel joy when we learn that our insurance rate is lower than what we thought it was going to be. In each case, there is a change in either a potential or real outcome relative to what we expected. Table 2.1 summarizes the relationship between the factors that drive emotions and the specific emotion we are likely to experience.

When the reward is greater than we expected or the punishment is less than we anticipated, we experience positive emotions, while the opposite produces negative emotions. Changes in outcomes often engender a feeling of (positive or negative) surprise. If we are certain of a better reward than we previously expected, we experience joy, relief, and gratitude. When we experience a loss that is difficult to cope with, we feel sad, desolate, and hurt.

Table 2.1 Factors that drive emotions and their effects

Likelihood of Outcome	Positive Emotions		Negative Emotions		Ability to Cope
	Better than Expected		Worse than Expected		
	Reward	Punishment	Reward	Punishment	
Unexpected	Surprise				
Uncertain	Hope		Fear/anxiety		Difficult
Certain	Joy	Relief	Sadness	Distress/disgust	Difficult
Uncertain	Hope		Frustration/anxiety		Easy
Certain	Joy	Relief	Frustration		Easy

The degree of uncertainty of an outcome substantially influences the emotions we experience. If there is a possibility of an improvement in an outcome but we are not sure if it will occur, we feel hope. For example, if you are on a waiting list for an upgrade to a service and you see that you've reached the top of the list, you are filled with expectation. If we sense that an outcome may be worse than we expected and difficult to cope with, we feel dread. The onset of a dull chest pain induces fear in persons in their late fifties, with or without a history of heart disease. The specific nature of the emotions also depends on the significance of the goal. Searching for your car keys in the morning is merely frustrating because the potential loss is not very significant and easy to cope with. On the other hand, the cancellation of an insurance policy because of an error by the carrier can generate fury.

Customers perceive service encounters as inherently risky and commonly manifest anxiety and worry during service delivery. This is largely the result of the individual nature of service transactions themselves, making each one a little different from all previous ones. Although the transaction is informed by past experience, we also know that we can gauge the quality of the service only after we utilize or consume it.

The specific emotions we feel also depend on who was responsible for the change in outcome. If we are responsible for an improvement, we feel pride. If the improvement is the result of someone else's

Table 2.2 Emotions experienced based upon source of change

Caused by	Positive Emotions	Negative Emotions	Ability to Cope
	Reward/Better than Expected	Punishment/Worse than Expected	
Others	Like	Dislike	Easy
Others	Like	Anger	Difficult
Self	Pride	Shame, guilt	Easy
Self	Pride	Regret, anger	Difficult

action, we begin to like that individual or entity. Table 2.2 lists the emotional nuances we typically feel based on the source of the change.

While this may seem like a lot of detail, the information provided is of value. The value of appraisal theory is its natural link to process flows. We can map emotions into flowcharts of service encounters. The boxed example illustrates this connection.

First-Time Home Buyers

According to Ms. B. Uzemeck, a Realtor in Southern California, most first-time home buyers go through a series of predictable emotions during the purchase cycle. When they start the process, they are usually anxious about whether they will qualify for a loan and whether they will find a house that they like in their price range. Once they qualify for a loan, they experience a mixture of relief, joy, and pride. If they see a house that they like but for some reason they are not able to close the deal, they are going to experience disappointment, frustration, or anger. If they are finally able to close a deal on the house they want, they are filled with joy. Most of Uzemeck's customers recognize that she plays a very significant role in finding their home, and, as a result, she is well liked. A large percentage of her customers continue to stay in contact with her decades after they purchase their homes.

Employing the appraisal theory framework, we can classify the encounters themselves. Figure 2.2 maps some service encounters along the following two dimensions:

- Whether the encounter induces positive or negative emotions

- Significance of the encounter to the customer and/or the ability of the customer to cope with the outcome

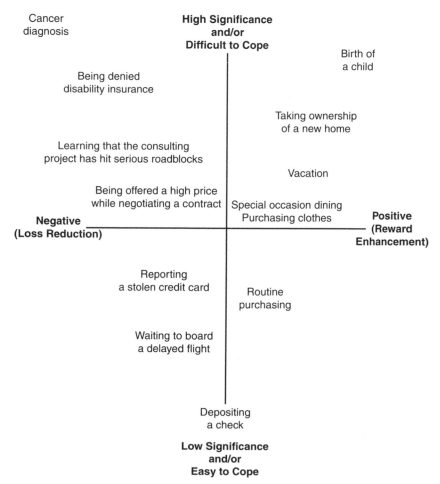

Figure 2.2 Types of emotions and significance of different encounters

TIERED APPROACH FOR SHAPING EMOTIONS

Appraisal theory links service activities and emotions. It enables us to anticipate the emotions that customers are likely to experience at different stages in the process. We can also anticipate customer emotions based on their transaction history and the segment they belong to. For example, a customer calling a clinic to find out the results of his HIV test is in all likelihood going to be feeling stressed. Air passengers heading for vacation are typically experiencing different feelings from those traveling for business. By carefully applying concepts of appraisal theory, companies can design nimble service systems that anticipate customer feelings and deliver the appropriate responses. Empathy is key to good service because it means that the provider knows how the customer feels.

In addition to reacting properly to customer feelings, firms can also proactively manage them. For example, if the managers at an urgent care facility already know that waiting customers begin to lose patience after 30 minutes, a service agent can approach a waiting customer after 20 minutes, apologize for the delay, and offer an explanation. Concert organizers at Rock in Rio build anticipation and whip the impatient crowd into a frenzy that peaks just as the featured rock star shows up on stage. These examples illustrate the way savvy firms can use the link between process flows and emotions to mitigate negative feelings and accentuate the positive ones.

Really savvy firms do even more. Service firms can differentiate themselves from the competition based on the emotions that they want customers to associate with their brand and to experience in the service encounter. Like Kaiser Permanente's Thrive campaign, firms require an overall branding strategy in order to leverage the value of emotions. Kaiser Permanente chose optimism (hope), confidence, pride, determination, and enthusiasm. It designed processes, ads, decor, and employee training that deliver these emotions. Such a comprehensive approach can be viewed in tiers.

Tier 1: Strategy

At the highest level, the firm or a business unit defines its strategy by selecting an image and overall *emotional theme* for its brand. The emotional theme constitutes a framework for determining the appropriate choice of people (employees), processes, products, and physical assets utilized by the firm. Alternatively, a company might want to apply feelings more narrowly, perhaps restricted to a single business unit or subset of its services. Certainly, a healthcare provider is likely to pursue one set of emotions in its birthing center and another in the hospice unit.

Tier 2: Tactics

At the second level, service providers deploy the emotional theme throughout every interaction. To do so, they must identify, evaluate, and act on three components:

- Service cycles using appraisal theory to determine the points at which customers are likely to experience emotions, developing appropriate responses, perhaps even developing an entirely new set of activities

- Process steps in which negative emotions are likely to be experienced—which may depend on the transaction history of the customer segment—and developing mechanisms to proactively mitigate them

- Process steps in which positive emotions are likely to be experienced, exploring ways to build anticipation

DESIGNING EMOTIONAL THEMES

Many entertainment, sports, and hospitality companies execute emotional themes very well. Disney designs every encounter to create a "magical experience." Southwest Airlines explicitly and consistently touts "love" as the company's central emotional theme. The emotional theme need not be the same in every part of the business, however. Marriott Hotels & Resorts offers "a world of opportunity" while the parent company, Marriott International, "opens doors of opportunity" through its many brands.

A note of caution: emotional themes need not be the elemental emotions identified through appraisal theory. These themes need to be meaningful for the customer in terms of the service being delivered. They can connote a range of feelings, preferably consistent with a wide range of employee behaviors and system designs. Allstate's tag line, "You're in good hands," is meaningful to customers buying automobile or home insurance policies. They expect the behavior of agents responding to claims to be consistent with it; that is, warm and caring or calm and sincere.

A leading German automotive manufacturer, interested in car sharing services, wanted to give the new business a sporty image. "Sporty" evokes a range of images and feelings, including action, dynamism, health, positivity, competitiveness, energy, diving to save a goal, primal energy, muscularity, and fitness. To realize this theme, a coherent subset of these impressions must first be distilled. Next, management would need to agree on the behaviors and images that are consistent with the chosen feelings. Finally, managers would develop service products, processes, and interactions that demonstrate the theme.

Themed Hospitality

One of the great emotional theme innovators, Joie de Vivre Hospitality, operates 28 boutique hotels in the San Francisco Bay area. Each hotel takes its emotional theme from a different popular magazine, with the ambiance of the building embodying it. Hotel Vitale in San Francisco, for example, pursues women business travelers and uses *Country Living* magazine to set the emotional tone for its facilities and amenities. The hotel decor is modern with waterfall walls in the lobby and flowers throughout. The rooms have soft lighting, muted tones, and modernistic pictures on the wall. Hotel staff members display a warm, upbeat attitude.

Vitale (or *vital*) means "abundant physical and mental energy usually combined with a wholehearted and joyous approach to situations and activities." In that spirit, the hotel heavily promotes its spa and early morning yoga classes on a rooftop overlooking the bay. In order to reduce feelings of anxiety about getting to meetings in San Francisco, a key task of the hotel staff is facilitating guest logistics, which includes providing courtesy cars so that no one has to wait for a ride.

The Phoenix Hotel, another Joie de Vivre property, designs its emotional experience around *Rolling Stone* magazine in its pursuit of guests from the rock music community. Located in a remodeled 1960s motel at the edge of San Francisco's Tenderloin, the Phoenix Hotel sells an emotional platform of hip, high spirits. Every page of its website attests to that image, inviting a certain kind of traveler to the party with, "This could be your ticket to hanging poolside with the likes of Radiohead or Sonic Youth," and "Our colorful front desk staff (who wouldn't be caught dead at the front desk of a Ritz-Carlton) is truly knowledgeable about the city's hidden treasures—including a party tonight that might just be right for you. The Phoenix is your way of getting connected with what's going on locally."

The Joie de Vivre website also offers the hotel matchmaker, which is a five-item test to help prospective guests select the specialty hotel that best suits their explicit preferences and thus meets their implicit emotional needs (see Figure 2.3).

In the restaurant business, Mike Simms, one of the owners of a rapidly growing chain of themed restaurants selects the theme based on where he would like to eat and the emotional ambience it conveys. Simmzy's in Manhattan Beach, California, is a bar restaurant that has simple home food and is designed as "my man cave," since Mike has five females in his family and likes the ambience of a sports bar "hangout." Another is the Lazy Dog Saloon (now in several locations), which is an authentic reproduction of a cowboy

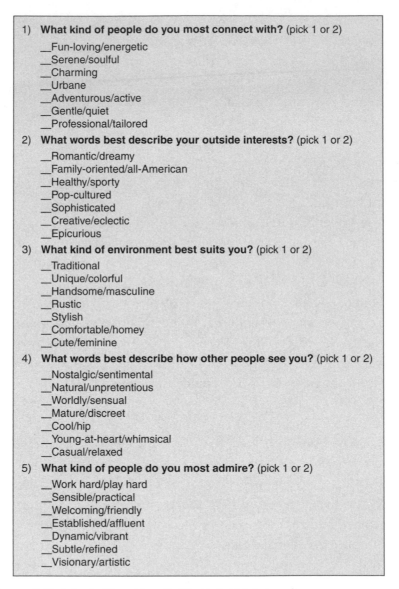

1) **What kind of people do you most connect with?** (pick 1 or 2)
___Fun-loving/energetic
___Serene/soulful
___Charming
___Urbane
___Adventurous/active
___Gentle/quiet
___Professional/tailored

2) **What words best describe your outside interests?** (pick 1 or 2)
___Romantic/dreamy
___Family-oriented/all-American
___Healthy/sporty
___Pop-cultured
___Sophisticated
___Creative/eclectic
___Epicurious

3) **What kind of environment best suits you?** (pick 1 or 2)
___Traditional
___Unique/colorful
___Handsome/masculine
___Rustic
___Stylish
___Comfortable/homey
___Cute/feminine

4) **What words best describe how other people see you?** (pick 1 or 2)
___Nostalgic/sentimental
___Natural/unpretentious
___Worldly/sensual
___Mature/discreet
___Cool/hip
___Young-at-heart/whimsical
___Casual/relaxed

5) **What kind of people do you most admire?** (pick 1 or 2)
___Work hard/play hard
___Sensible/practical
___Welcoming/friendly
___Established/affluent
___Dynamic/vibrant
___Subtle/refined
___Visionary/artistic

Figure 2.3 Joie de Vivre Hospitality Hotel Matchmaker
Source: © 2003 Joie de Vivre Hospitality.

bar that one would find in a lodge in Wyoming. The Lazy Dog name comes from the owner commenting that he would like the place to convey the relaxed contentment of "that lazy dog over there" resting by the fire.

Lost in a Crystal Landscape

Swarovski, maker of luxury cut crystal near Innsbruck, Austria, has created an experience to define the brand. Swarovski Kristallwelten (Crystal Worlds) is a theme park that blends retailing with a garden, theater, and museum of astonishing crystal installations. Its director, Stefan Isser, describes the park as an escape into a surreal world made of crystal. Really, it's much more than that, combining haute cuisine, art, history, music, and massive crystal environments into a sometimes overwhelming experience. Some exhibits connect with ancient myths and legends; others, like a geodesic dome made of mirrors to create the feeling of being inside a crystal, create unique visual experiences. Whereas most theme parks deliver a defined experience, Crystal Worlds tries to develop and communicate the brand through an experience.

One Theme Says It All

For Reno's world-famous Harrah's casino, the logical emotional theme might seem to be fun and excitement. Management discovered, however, that their most valued customers attach the utmost significance to feeling lucky when they choose which casino to visit. Though nothing makes us feel luckier than winning, the chances of winning and the amount paid out depend on the odds in that game—blackjack, slots, craps, roulette—all of which favor the casinos. Skill is a real factor in only a few games such as poker.

Harrah's nevertheless knows what creates a lucky feeling. It knows that gamblers are superstitious and believe in routines and rituals. Everything from the availability of favorite parking spots and slot machines to employee friendliness to wait times to dine or cash-in tokens affects their sense of luck. Gamblers also like to hear the satisfying clink of slot machines paying out.

What gamblers hate is waiting. When they're winning, any delay threatens their good luck. So that customers on a roll can avoid impediments, Harrah's makes it a priority to prevent waits while checking into the hotel, getting chips, or being seated in the restaurants. Today, if you win a jackpot at Harrah's, you'll have someone there to help within 90 seconds. Other hotels on the Strip can make you wait 10 minutes or more.

Harrah's also delivers personalized and responsive customer service through its loyalty program. It offers tailored services for regular customers, such as supplying shop floor employees educated in their gambling obsessions and idiosyncrasies, providing separate waiting lines in the restaurants, and ensuring access to their favorite machines, parking spots, and rooms. They track frequent patrons, and when one embarks on an extended period of losing, a Harrah's manager interrupts the game and takes the guest out for a meal on the house, thus helping break a "streak of bad luck."

Harrah's commitment to fostering a sense of good luck has paid off handsomely, allowing parent company Harrah's Entertainment, Inc., to buy out one of its main competitors in 2005, Caesars Entertainment. The parent company name has since reverted to the more famous one, with Harrah's as a key brand, but it's still calling on lady luck, as confirmed by "Feeling Lucky 2012," a recent travel agent incentive program.

Well-Executed Plays

Another industry that does a good job of incorporating emotional themes is professional sports. Central to a good sporting experience is the adrenaline flow of a crowd electrified by the emotional roller coaster of the game. The more the fans identify with the teams, the greater the personal stake in the outcome and the more dramatic the range of emotional highs and lows. Cheerleaders, crowd enthusiasm, sports memorabilia, even the national anthem feed that primitive need to belong to a tribe, all of which increases the significance of the game. Teams pump up the importance of a game with the pomp and pageantry of pregame shows, glorifying video, sound effects, and even fighter jet flyovers.

The affiliation that fans feel for their teams transcends overt cognitive processes and often bleeds into near insanity (hence the derivation of the word *fan* from *fanatic*). European soccer matches are notorious for rioting fans. In the United States, morbidity statistics are maintained for Super Bowl game days. Even the run up to the Super Bowl is hazardous, as in the case of a Pittsburgh Steelers fan who suffered a heart attack when star running back Jerome Bettis fumbled the ball toward the end of the January 2006 AFC championship game against the Indianapolis Colts. Imagine how closely that fan identified with the Steelers.

Outside of a few industries, we find that firms don't pay much attention to the emotional theme they are creating for their customers. An argument could be made for the retail sector in that the physical setting of the store is designed to create the desired feelings. This attention to impact, however, seldom carries down to the type of personnel employed and their training and guidance concerning the emotional tone of customer/personnel interactions. The healthcare sector is one of the worst when it comes to delivering emotionally sensitive customer service. Given the consequence of healthcare transactions and the emotional significance they have for the patients, healthcare managers would do well to examine the emotional themes their organizations create by default, consider the emotions they might do well to foster, and institute new processes to effect positive change.

Case Study in Customer Experience Design

As in gambling, nothing improves on the sports experience more than winning, yet there's little anyone other than athletes in the arena can do to improve the odds or influence the outcome. But Pete Winemiller, who has been an NBA franchise executive for 18 years, was a vice president of guest relations with the Seattle Sonics, and is now a senior vice president of guest relations for the Oklahoma City Thunder, understands sports fans. He realized that athletic play is just one part of the drama contributing to the energy at the game, and thanks to a departmental revamp in line with his and his management team's insights, the Sonics had for some time one of the highest retention rates for season ticket buyers in the NBA despite a less than stellar record.

Winemiller continues to employ his approach with the Thunder by focusing guest relations efforts on making the Thunder "the most fan-centric organization in pro sports." In 2008, Winemiller and his staff led the implementation of a customer service program in the inaugural season of the Oklahoma franchise, under what Commissioner Stern called, "The most compressed beginning ever in professional sports." His efforts were so effective that in a very short time the Thunder has developed an award-winning service operation. Through Winemiller, the Thunder organization recognized that personal contact strengthens the emotional bond between the customers and the franchise. The Thunder's emotional theme incorporated a consistent "attitude of invitation" by behaving like a host welcoming its guests to the game. Major components of its successful strategy incorporated targeted staff training:

- Contact staff to welcome and assist fans attending the game

- Customer service representatives to build relationships with season ticket holders

CREATING PROCESSES TO DELIVER
THE EMOTIONAL THEME

Possessing an emotional theme limits the range of options and thus simplifies employee and facility selection and process design. Harrah's managers were surprised to discover that, with luck as the company's emotional platform, casino decor didn't need to be opulent. They found that their gambling clientele regarded some of the company's older properties to be luckier sites, described as having more "character" than the newer ones. That's when they shifted their emphasis to segmenting customers based on their usage and ensuring that they sustained a perception of luck.

To that end, Harrah's redesigned its service delivery system to help gamblers maintain their rituals and to eliminate any negative vibes caused by extended waits or rude casino employees. Members of management identified friendliness and helpfulness as the key treatment dimensions, and they explicitly evaluate employee performance in those areas every day. They instituted an incentive system that individually allocates annual employee raises based upon the person exceeding the previous year's performance.

In addition, high-tech data networks facilitate service delivery. Employees on the floor can quickly access a wide range of preferences expressed by top customers. Slot machines use Harrah's preferred customer cards, which change the color of the lights on the top to indicate the status of the person playing. This makes it easier for employees to offer tiered services. Frequent visitors also have separate lines for check-in, meals, and selected vending machines.

The problems faced by the Oklahoma City Thunder at the service delivery level were particularly challenging because only about 50 of the 600 employees worked for the organization full time. The rest, working at the games as ushers, vendors, cooks, and maintenance staff, were subcontractors employed by other companies. Nonetheless, Pete Winemiller's team made sure that every part-time and temporary employee was educated in the nuances of displaying the desired "attitude of invitation." During orientation to the Thunder organization, each person was asked to select the behavior that felt most comfortable. Employees at all levels quickly realized the importance of maintaining eye contact, kneeling to talk to children, smiling, and performing small, gracious acts. As a reminder, each contact employee wore a plastic card with the word CLICK, which stands for:

Communicate courteously

Listen to learn

Initiate immediately

Create connections

Know your stuff

When management spotted employees "clicking" with a guest, employees were given a CLICK! chip, which they could redeem for a gift at the fan information booth.

In mass services like these, continued employee reinforcement is paramount; one or two negative customer events can ruin the experience for many. This focused service approach of being inviting makes service delivery simpler and at the same time reduces the burden of emotional labor. The approach Winemiller developed can readily be generalized to other attitudes, such as an attitude of caring, encouragement, or celebration.

Pumping Up the Energy

If you go to the Chesapeake Energy Arena, where the Oklahoma City Thunder rule, for a professional basketball game you might notice a fellow sitting at a courtside table wearing a headset and working several computers. Though his job title is director of events and entertainment, he has nothing to do with managing the team or operating the arena. Instead, he directs the show happening on the court. He controls the timing of scripted events that take place during timeouts, commercial breaks, breaks between quarters, and halftime. He controls much of the fan involvement and energy level during the game by flashing "D-Fence," "Charge," and "Noise" on the huge overhead screens, where he also runs player clips and instant replays.

BLUEPRINTS FOR TRACKING YOUR CUSTOMERS' EMOTIONS

Companies dedicated to managing emotions must anticipate the emotions customers are likely to experience during service encounters and identify emotions likely to arise at different stages of the encounter. Flowcharts and blueprints used to map service processes can also help locate points at which outcomes, whether real or anticipated, are going to change or are going to be communicated to the customer. Appraisal theory tells us that these are the points that are likely to generate emotions. With that information, we can associate potential emotional responses from customers at each stage of the process. Being aware of these triggers creates an opportunity for the organization to be proactive and minimize negative feelings while accentuating positive ones.

Consider a customer whose car has just broken down. The blueprint for the automotive service process is laid out in Figure 2.4.

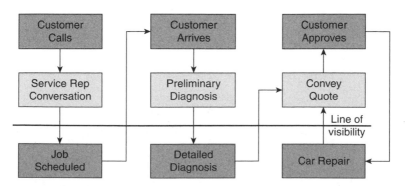

Figure 2.4 Service blueprint indicating the limit of the customer's view

A line of visibility separates the events in which the customer actually participates and the unseen, back office events and decisions by the repair facility employees. Above the line are the call, arrival, greeting, conversations, and closing in which the customer participates. Below the line are the discussions, decisions, research, and repair activities of the shop staff.

Emotionprints

According to appraisal theory, customers are primed to display various emotions at each decision stage in the service blueprint. We can plot these emotions and track them on a graph we call the *emotionprint*, as illustrated in Figure 2.5. In our example, the customer doesn't know what caused the problem or how bad it is. The car simply wouldn't start that morning, so he called the repair shop which towed the car in, while the customer caught a ride to work with his wife.

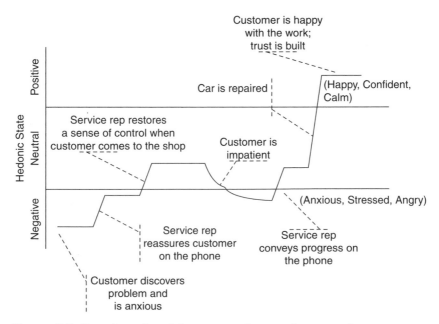

Figure 2.5 Emotionprint of the automotive repair encounter

Changes in the customer's emotional state are going to correspond to information he receives or delays he encounters as he deals with employees at the shop. To start with, he's frustrated and angry at the unwelcome surprise before work. Then there's his uncertainty about the nature of the problem, which translates to anxiety. By anticipating the customer's feelings, the shop's service rep can take steps to dispel them by greeting the customer sympathetically and conveying the shop's competence. The staff mechanics can help diffuse some of the anxiety by offering the preliminary diagnosis in such a way that the customer perceives a measure of control, has clear choices, and confirms his wisdom at turning his vehicle over to this shop.

Now the shop performs a detailed diagnosis. At this stage, delays in communicating with the customer or providing the detailed quote are going to elicit more worry or anger, depending on the magnitude of the problem. Delays also increase customer uncertainty and the perception of risk. The customer may begin to worry about the cost of fixing the car and the competence and motivation of the repair facility.

Many auto repair shops have built loyal customer bases without realizing that they partly owe their success to the emotional intelligence of their staff. In such cases, employee turnover can be disastrous. By anticipating potential emotional responses, however, organizations can develop guidelines for all employee interactions with customers. It can be a simple matter of training staff to distinguish the necessary information, to understand how to communicate it, and to recognize when to notify customers about changes or delays. Appraisal theory shows that anxiety is caused by uncertainty, and the depth of the feeling depends on the seriousness of the problem and the customer's perception of control and capacity for coping with the issue. To lighten the situation, employees can provide substantive information quickly thereby addressing the primary source of uncertainty. It may also be possible to frame the scope of the problem in a way that makes it easier for the customer to cope with it.

Emotionprint Applicability

We have found the emotionprint approach to mapping the course of feelings useful when designing extended services such as those involved in obstetrics practices, in-patient surgeries, real estate transactions (especially home-buying experiences), and engineering and consulting projects. Customers making use of obstetric services, for example, vary according to many factors, including age, number of pregnancies, complications, family situation, and income status. Experienced obstetricians could easily lay out multiple workflows for every condition and contingency, overlay an emotionprint on each one, and proactively develop the appropriate responses. From that, the entire obstetrics office can learn to help manage patients' feelings as they arise at every stage.

For example, consider the routine ultrasound conducted for a pregnancy. When a woman is expecting a child, she typically feels a combination of joy and anxiety. Assuming the pregnancy is uncomplicated, the ultrasound is a high point with new parents ultimately finding the procedure to be a joyful and memorable event. Of course, sound medical concerns prompt the procedure and incite some worry. By using an emotionprint, medical staff members can improve the overall experience by anticipating, recognizing, and addressing the feelings even while they provide the necessary information. An ultrasound that produces normal findings could incorporate a simple celebration. By punctuating the peak emotional event, the obstetrics staff also helps prepare the patient for a positive delivery experience—an event most women find scary—by reinforcing the positive emotional theme of, "We're with you all the way."

Bariatric patients anticipating a surgical procedure for obesity tend to feel a very different constellation of emotions, including helplessness, anxiety, shame, frustration, hope, and relief. Patients typically maintain contact with the surgeon for nearly six months, allowing considerable time beforehand for testing and working to improve their health. Understanding how patients feel throughout the ordeal and increasing compliance with a strict health regimen remain an open problem. Surgeons as a professional group are known more for their confidence than their empathy. Though the work flow tends to be straightforward—even as to the potential for crises—the anticipation of patient emotions at the various stages is often neglected.

Healthcare organizations committed to improving patient outcomes would be well-advised to attend to their patients' emotional states while they are attending to the biochemical, structural, and mechanical ones. They should also heed the emotional needs of patients' support system, especially the family.

Attending to Anxious Relatives

Hospital staff members know that concerned family members are likely to accompany patients to admissions on the day of surgery. Even with federal privacy permissions in place, hours have been known to pass before family members received a single update. They often don't know that, after the patient goes into pre-op, the procedure might not start for another hour or two. It's a fairly simple matter to include mechanisms for keeping the family informed. Clinical staff members can be trained to associate time-delimited care activities with the likely emotional states and needs of both the patient (while conscious) and the waiting family.

White Memorial Hospital in Los Angeles has implemented a radio frequency–based system to track patients. The system supplies data that the staff uses to inform family members about their loved one's status.

Extended services are often complex because a number of processes that work in parallel involve multiple service providers and customers. At the same time, systematically charting the work flows and understanding the emotions likely to occur at each stage are definitely warranted. Just as process analysis was central to improving production systems in the 1980s, charting emotions will allow organizations to improve the quality of their customers' experiences.

Emotionprinting is a straightforward procedure that is easy to implement. Since high emotions create memories that are retained for a long time, knowing and addressing them pays off in many ways and helps create loyal customers.

Tweeting for Reaction

The Los Angeles Kings, winners of the 2012 Stanley Cup, used Twitter to raise the emotional temperature of their fan base. After beating the Vancouver Canucks in the playoffs, the Kings tweeted, "To everyone in Canada outside of BC. You are welcome." This obviously did not sit well with Canuck fans, but it created a huge buzz among hockey fans everywhere else. Mike Altieri, LA Kings vice president of communications and broadcasting, explained his group's position while making the official apology. "We encourage our digital team to be creative, interactive, and to apply a sense of humor whenever possible," he said. "To anyone who found it offensive, we sincerely apologize."

Then, sounding like a graduate of the Pete Winemiller School of Guest Relations, he continued to say, "It's definitely a philosophical approach we choose to take. We believe engagement is first and foremost in all our digital strategies because we feel . . . engagement [brings us the] types of things we want for our business, for our organization over time."[7] In sports it is all about the involvement and emotions—the stronger the better to create memorable experiences.

SEGMENTING YOUR CUSTOMERS

Clearly, different challenges distress different people in different ways. This means that if we are to provide emotionally responsive services, task and treatment protocols should be sensitive to each customer's personality. This is a good time to take a deep breath.

We fully grasp the difficulty of identifying and responding to personality differences as a matter of routine. All you really need to do, however, is segment customers into a limited number of tiers according to a simple demographic profile that can be associated with the tasks they require and the emotional states that can be anticipated at each stage. Consider the obstetrics example we presented earlier. We stated that four easily determined factors indicate a limited number of emotional responses:

- Patient age

- Complexity of the pregnancy

- Number of previous pregnancies

- Social support available to the patient

Another example comes from the insurance industry, which collects masses of data to compile actuarial tables and other risk charts. A firm providing health insurance to Americans working for multinational firms in Southeast Asia found that the emotions customers displayed depended on three customer factors:

- Age

- Family composition

- Length of time lived abroad

In obstetrics and insurance, these statistics are readily available for segmenting the customer populations into tiers according to services required, work flow associated, and emotions likely to emerge along the way.

In some services, customers reveal their segments through their choices. According to Derrick Hall, CEO of the Arizona Diamondbacks, the team's fans run the gamut from families with young children to fans who want to party during the game. Chase Field in Phoenix, home of the Diamondbacks, serves both groups, with playgrounds for kids in one part of the stadium and bars and restaurants in another part. The service and emotional theme in each segment is tailored accordingly, and customers reveal their preferences by way of their seat selections.

When services are provided by a call center or over the Internet, detecting the customer segment or the type of service the customer needs is relatively straightforward. Call centers can use caller ID or call triaging to channel the customer to the appropriate agent. Websites apply customer profile information to each encounter and tailor the language, nature of the conversation, and physical attributes of the website to the emotional theme.

RESPONDING TO YOUR CUSTOMERS' TRANSACTION HISTORY

Traditional customer relationship management (CRM) systems track customer purchase patterns to identify opportunities for increasing sales or reducing defections. Historical transaction data is a valuable resource that also can be applied to managing emotions. Prior history can be used to anticipate the emotional state of the caller. For instance, if we know that the customer is calling about a stock trade and her last few calls were handled well, we can expect her disposition to be positive. Conversely, if we're able to predict that a caller is going to be angry, then the agent can be informed about the transaction history and alerted to the customer's likely emotional state. Knowing that the caller is upset will enable the agent to prepare her response and recognize that the anger is not directed at her. The call center can also leverage its most emotionally intelligent employees by rerouting the call to those especially skilled at handling complaints.

In the case of the obstetrics practice, the staff should be trained to interact with patients in a particularly sensitive manner when the news from an ultrasound or genetic test is negative. Again, distressing news is best handled by persons with the aptitude and the training to service such patients, and it's crucial in such cases that these sensitive handlers include the medical staff.

A LIMITED APPROACH TO MANAGING EMOTIONS

Customer emotions are particularly high when there is a failure. You are not amused when the dry cleaner loses your shirt or the call center drops your phone call during a transfer. Firms have recognized the importance of service recovery and discovered that good service recovery can actually bolster loyalty. This finding illustrates the importance of recognizing and properly responding to emotional moments during an encounter. A more limited approach to managing emotions could be to focus only on interactions that generate the strongest feelings. Consistent with appraisal theory, we can group these moments into four categories: the service provider is responsible or not responsible for the emotions; and the emotions are positive or negative.

Service recovery, which we discuss in Chapter 7, "Attribution," is needed when the firm is responsible for negative emotions. Regardless of who arouses emotions, firms have an opportunity to build a relationship. For instance, when customers call the insurance company after a car accident, they are stressed, but for reasons not caused by the firm. The agent knows this and has an opportunity to parlay that awareness into an emotional bond by being supportive and guiding the customer through the claim process. Figure 2.6 summarizes strategies available in each of the four situations.

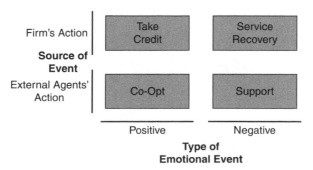

Figure 2.6 Strategies for dealing with emotional moments

KEY PRINCIPLES FOR DESIGNING FOR OPTIMAL EMOTIONAL IMPACT

"Keep emotions out of it" is really one of the hardest admonitions to follow in service encounters, so no matter what the service is, you want to manage emotions in light of their inevitable existence. Here are some principles that help in doing this:

1. **Think in terms of an emotional platform.** This can be at the same level of strategic importance as the service product or, indeed, the brand itself.

2. **Think of emotions as flowing in parallel with activities that occur at each stage of your business.** People are likely to have different emotions while they are waiting for service, partaking of the service, and leaving the service, so you need to plan accordingly. Emotionprints can be used to show how the emotions flow.

3. **Think in terms of customer histories and how they influence customer emotions.** Far too many services are memoryless when it comes to past customer interactions. Simply keeping track of what happened in a previous call to a call center can give a clue to the customer's likely emotions in the next call.

4. **Think in terms of attribution theory when dealing with emotional situations.** Remember the four actions that a company rep can take when a good thing or a bad thing happens to a customer as a function of the source of the event (you or the other guy)—Good thing: take credit, co-opt; Bad thing: service recovery, support.

CONCLUSION

Emotions that customers experience during a service encounter affect their response to the service provider and their recollection of the events. The defining moments during an encounter are almost always associated with strong feelings. Emotional bonding between a customer and a firm is now being recognized as a basis for loyalty.

We propose a two-stage approach for firms committed to systematically managing customer emotions. First, identifying the desired key emotional theme frames the emotion the service provider wants to engender. This decision informs personnel selection, training, and detailed process design. Second, work flow and process blueprints can be augmented to create an emotionprint that tracks emotions that customers typically experience at each stage. Emotionprints allow firms to engineer emotionally sensitive responses at the process level.

Given the increasing trend of relying on technology and offshoring to deliver services, incorporating emotionally appropriate responses into process specifications makes eminent sense but immediately inspires questions about the emotional authenticity of the response. Systematic planning up front allows firms to minimize this problem. For one thing, anticipating emotions enables firms to reduce the possibility of negative events. For another, making staff members aware of potential emotional states offers a greater likelihood of generating empathy. The firm can also use available scientific expertise to articulate proper responses, including when and how to escalate a problem. Finally, a company can apply the information to employee selection and training.

3

ENGENDERING YOUR CUSTOMERS' TRUST

In the Disney version of the ancient tale, Aladdin is trapped on a Baghdad rooftop with the princess. He signals the princess to jump on the magic carpet, but she hesitates. So he asks her, "Do you trust me?"

In services, customers often have to make a leap of faith too.

All service encounters are predicated on trusting the service organization to perform its function as advertised. We trust the restaurant to keep a clean kitchen. We trust the doctor to give us a correct diagnosis and adhere to the correct protocol when treating an illness. We trust the tax preparer to keep us from being audited. We trust that the amusement park rides are safe. We trust that we're "in good hands" with Allstate and that the price of its insurance policy is fair. We trust the taxi driver to take the shortest route from the airport to the hotel. We trust the rock concert producers to create an unforgettable event. We hope that the divorce lawyer is acting in the best interest of the client. The list goes on and on.

There are times we should be considerably more skeptical and perform our due diligence before we surrender control. To demonstrate, we look at a case very close to home. Twenty years ago, I (Sriram) had knee surgery to remove some torn cartilage. It started with a nagging pain in my left knee that forced me to see my primary care physician, who referred me to a sports medicine specialist. The sport medicine specialist examined the MRI and concluded that I was suffering from avascular necrosis, a very ominous-sounding diagnosis. The specialist scheduled me with a surgeon and told me to use crutches, putting no weight on my left leg until after the surgery. I was on crutches for nearly seven weeks, and, in that period, my left leg atrophied considerably. The surgeon was the top orthopedic surgeon at UCLA, with a client list that included professional athletes. This gave me some comfort, which I needed because his bedside manner left a lot to be desired. A colleague of mine who was also his patient suggested that I ask for local anesthesia and observe the surgery on a television monitor. I followed my friend's advice, but the surgery turned out to be very painful, and I asked for general anesthesia as soon as the surgery began.

Over the years I have learned from other physicians that my particular surgical procedure always entails considerable pain and requires general anesthesia. What's worse, it turned out that I didn't have avascular necrosis and that I should not have depended on crutches for such an extended period. Two decades later, my leg hasn't fully recovered. I don't know if the diagnosis error was avoidable. I probably should have gotten a second opinion. I also confess that I should have more diligently adhered to the rehab regimen.

MARKET MECHANISMS FOR REDUCING RISK FOR YOUR CUSTOMER

The example highlights some tricky issues involved in trust. Customers employ service providers for their skills, resources, and knowledge. At the same time, customers don't have the technical knowledge or skill to thoroughly evaluate the capabilities of most service providers. In fact, they have only a limited understanding of what needs to be done, what is being done, and later, as in my surgery, what the quality of the job was. On the other hand, service providers themselves do not always fully control the outcome. Also, customer actions may contribute to the outcome. The prevalence of these concerns has resulted in a number of mechanisms to reduce the risks to customers. Taxi companies have a minimum fixed fare and variable rate that starts after a few miles. This payment structure reduces the incentive for a taxi driver to cheat.[1]

Service delivery is typically partitioned into two components, both requiring trust but the second containing the veritable leap of faith (commitment) on the part of the customer. The first phase is a diagnosis phase in which the provider tells the customer what needs to be done and how much it will cost. The second phase comprises all parts of the actual service delivery. During the first phase, a cancer patient may visit multiple oncologists before committing to a specific physician and treatment plan in the second phase. Similarly, a homeowner embarking on a remodeling plan obtains multiple quotes before selecting a general contractor. The diagnosis phase serves as a valuable learning opportunity for the customer and reduces some of the asymmetry in knowledge between customer and service provider.

The parties may draw up a payment plan contingent on outcomes or performance. In a home remodeling project, the customer generally pays in multiple installments, with a significant percentage paid at the end, once he or she is satisfied with the outcome. Sometimes a third party acts as the agent of the buyer, as in real estate transactions where an escrow company makes sure that title deeds and insurance and other ducks are all in a row before money changes hands. In healthcare, third parties include review boards, ombudsmen, and medical officers in insurance companies, which exercise a certain amount of oversight. In short, a number of contracting schemes and institutions work to reduce the risk that customers face, though many services continue to be fraught with peril.

BENEFITS OF TRUST

You can test drive a new car, and if you don't like the feel, you don't have to buy it. You can buy a shirt from Nordstrom and return it later if you don't like how you look in it. On the other hand, you have little recourse in experiential service encounters. No matter how dissatisfied you are with a haircut, a surgery, a ten-day vacation in Greece, or four years at a university, you can't return it. In service industries, customers have to go through the consumption or delivery process in order to learn about the product. This represents a big risk; hence the reputation of the service provider has significant bearing on purchase decisions.

Company reputations are dictated by their brands, and the value of the brand depends on the level of trust customers have in the firm. Brand equity—its value—depends not only on name recognition but also on the regard customers have for the quality of service delivered by the firm.[2] For example, the Cleveland Clinic, consistently rated one of the nation's top hospitals, has a well-recognized name that connotes high-quality cardiac care. Brand equity increases customer loyalty, willingness to pay, and high customer lifetime value— expected profit from a customer's future business.[3]

In addition to the benefits of enhancing the relationship with the customer and generating positive word of mouth, trust brings a number of operational benefits to a given service encounter. If people trust you, you don't have to explain as much as you do when you are still building trust. Taking things on faith allows things to move along faster than when long explanations are needed. As the level of trust increases, customers are more comfortable ceding control, giving, for example, a trusted financial analyst a bit more latitude in designing their portfolio. Trust is a fund. Providers can bank high levels of trust and use them to diminish backlash in the event of a failure. Tom Brady, quarterback for the New England Patriots, has won three Super Bowl championships, so he can have a few bad games without his fan base getting restive.

COMPONENTS OF TRUST

We all have a general idea about trust, but like most concepts in this book, parsing the aspects of the term helps us use the concept to maximum effect. Obviously, the need for trust arises whenever there is risk, but if the risk can be avoided, there is no need for trust. As we saw earlier, real estate transactions in the United States don't require the buyer to trust the seller when it comes to the title deed. Nor does the seller have to trust the buyer with respect to his or her ability to pay for the property. The same transaction in India, however, would call for considerable trust between the seller and buyer.

An important factor in managing trust is to recognize that it involves taking a risk, making that "leap of faith." The reason someone is taking a risk is that the transaction combines some degree of vulnerability and uncertainty, which cannot be eliminated. The clients of divorce lawyers have to depend on the lawyer to determine the most effective and appropriate legal maneuvers. Clients of a retirement planner at Fidelity depend heavily on her to plot a secure path through myriad market uncertainties that may cloud her true intentions and capabilities.

The risks in the service relationship are rooted in the special expertise offered by the provider. Customers have to believe that the surgeon, mechanic, plumber, chef, management consultant, financial advisor, pilot, cruise ship captain, tour guide, or professor has the requisite skills and knowledge. First of all, we must be confident that the professor knows the subject, the financial advisor understands how options are priced, and the oncologist knows how to target a treatment based on the individual patient's genetics. Second, given all the uncertainties and lack of control over factors contributing to the outcome, we have to be convinced that, when a conflict of interest arises, the provider will act in our best interest. If there is a roadblock or an accident and a detour is needed, we expect the taxi driver to take the shortest route. We hope a financial advisor does not recommend a new mutual fund solely because of commissions. We hope the doctor does not insist on an expensive brand name drug instead of the generic version because she's affiliated with the pharmaceutical company. Thus, the risks are primarily associated with the provider's competence and motivation to act in the customer's best interest.

A third risk factor is the availability of the service provider. Customers count on the service provider to have the authority and sufficient resources to deliver the service. As dedicated and competent as the general contractor is, he may be spread too thin, juggling multiple remodeling jobs. The motivated and experienced airline agent who is trying to arrange an alternative flight after you missed a connection may not have the network access to make the changes or the authority to bump you up on the priority list.

While the server's competence, benevolence, and access to resources determine whether or not you get the best possible outcome, the willingness of the customer to trust the server depends on how the customer processes a plethora of cues. Customers trust a firm or a service employee if they are confident that the provider will act in their best interest, despite their inability to evaluate the server's resources and competence and the potential for opportunistic behavior.

WHOM DOES YOUR CUSTOMER TRUST: THE FIRM OR THE EMPLOYEE?

Customers may trust the service provider or firm, but in professional services such as healthcare, legal, and financial, the primary focus of trust is on the individual service agent. Moving away from relationship-based services to airlines, health insurance, towing services, restaurants, hotels, and universities, customers interact with many people and do so mostly through websites or by telephone. Here, too, customers may develop special relationships with a few employees, which doesn't necessarily translate to an affinity for the firm. The more global trust in a firm incorporates a customer's assessment of individual interactions with employees, either directly or anonymously, through e-mail, telephone conversations, or instant messaging. The customer blends that assessment with largely unarticulated perceptions of the policies and corporate culture that govern employee behavior.

We have a mostly positive view of service providers. You aren't going to be surprised to hear that the manager of the Hilton Hotel in Innsbruck was courteous to a fault and apologized that there was a problem with the shower. You'd also expect to hear that the shower was fixed right away, because that's been typical of Hilton management. In short, the default assumption is that the service will go well. The assessment implies that a rude or incompetent employee would be considered an exception rather than the rule. In a situation like the Innsbruck Hilton, you're going to recall lousy employees more vividly and talk about them more frequently. The good news, though, is that you aren't going to expect the same from other employees there. If you ran into another rude employee at another Hilton, however, the brand would be in serious jeopardy of losing you to another hospitality company.

The same sort of process occurs if you walk into a Wells Fargo branch and the manager greets you with a smile and asks you if there is anything he can do to help you. From that positive action, you are likely to assume that you'll receive the same treatment at other Wells Fargo branches. Positive behavior is more likely to be projected onto the firm.[4]

Many elements of service encounters are easily imputed to the firm in general. Satellite television provider DirecTV is constantly developing new promotional offers to attract customers, but these offers are not available to existing customers. When existing customers ask to participate, the request has historically been rejected, making the company appear cheap and ungrateful. Satellite contracts generally go for a mere two years, and as long as DirecTV has competition, it would be wise to foster customer loyalty.

Amazon.com was cited as the most trustworthy company in the United States (yet again) by respondents to a May 2012 survey on *Entrepreneur Magazine*'s website, Entrepreneur.com. First, Amazon rates high in all aspects of its core business of filling product orders. Second, it demonstrates motivation to serve through user reviews and ratings, recommending items based on past purchases, and suggesting complementary purchases. Third, it provides exceptional accessibility both online and by phone. All interactions with Amazon, like other web-based retailers, are impersonal and affect the firm's image, which, nonetheless, continues to be one of competence, friendliness, and reliability. At the other end of the trust spectrum, at least for the moment, sits American Airlines. When seats came loose on several American Airlines planes, customers reasonably assumed that a deep-rooted problem lay with management, that it was not the act of a disgruntled employee or result of spilled beverages (as claimed at one time).[5] Actions and outcomes that are attributed to systems, technology, websites, and policies directly impact trust in the firm.

MOMENTS THAT INFLUENCE TRUST

These are often called the "moments of truth" wherein the service company establishes its trustworthiness or reinforces it.

Initial Interactions

People are notoriously anxious when they embark on completely novel experiences. Each year approximately 180,000 visitors travel from the United States to New Zealand.[6] Approximately half of these visitors are tourists, and so we can reasonably assume that each year several thousand Americans are visiting New Zealand for the first time. You can almost hear the litany of fears:

How do we determine where to stay?

If we book a bed and breakfast online in the beautiful town of Kaikoura, are we being scammed?

Does the bed and breakfast really exist?

Are we subject to identity theft or credit card fraud?

These anxieties are unlikely to be shared by millions of visitors who have been there before or who are familiar with the websites. Predictably, whenever we go through a new experience or work with a new service provider, we pay more attention and anxiously calculate the trustworthiness of the service provider.

When Predicted Events Happen

New York University economics professor Nouriel Roubini is renowned for having predicted the 2008 market crash.[7] He gained prominence when his predictions came true, and now he's besieged with requests for more opinions. A similar effect is common to a wide range of service encounters. Brenda is an early childhood special educator who works with children experiencing developmental delays and with their parents. David, one of her clients, was a three-month-old with Down syndrome who was unable to hold his head up. This made it difficult for him to lie on his stomach, and unless babies spend time on their stomach, they don't develop the strength to lift their heads and become mobile. Brenda suggested that David's mother try rolling a towel and placing it under his chin, when he lay prone. She predicted that this simple but novel intervention would help David develop sufficient strength to hold his head up within two weeks. Indeed, shortly thereafter, David held his head up. When Brenda visited the family two weeks later, David's mother received her suggestions with much more enthusiasm than she had before, because her confidence in Brenda's knowledge had increased tremendously.

Here are a few more examples. Ariel is a tour guide in Maui who takes tourists kayaking and snorkeling. He knows a little bay where an octopus and a few sandbar sharks reside. When he delivers on a promise to show the children an octopus and a few sharks, the goodwill it generates for Ariel is very noticeable. Also, each time Flower.com delivers an order on time, trust in the firm grows, and if the map app on your smartphone underestimates travel times, you lose confidence in the tool. Each realized promise adds to the trust fund, and each failure depletes it. Happiness and gratitude enhance trust.

When Unexpected Events Happen

When customers are vulnerable and the firm is able to help them, confidence in the firm rises. This is true even when a customer's vulnerability is exaggerated by a penchant for anxiety. One of our friends was involved in a minor automobile accident, but was obsessively concerned about the consequences, terrified in fact. His AAA insurance agent worked hard to reassure him that, beyond the deductible, there would be no additional financial burden. He has been a loyal customer of AAA now for over a decade.

As we saw in our discussion on emotions, service failures generate strong feelings. In such cases, customers pay careful attention to the level of commitment their providers show for their welfare.[8] Unexpectedly good outcomes, such as when the Lexus service agent determines that the rattling sound is caused by a minor bearing misalignment, boost trust in the provider. Major negative events, such as the dislodging of seats in American Airlines aircrafts or gastrointestinal epidemics on Holland America Line cruises, attract considerable attention and concern from the general population.[9]

Vulnerability may also arise from events outside the control of the firm and the customer. Even so, when an American tourist loses a wallet to a pickpocket on a subway in Paris, France, the credit card company's response to this crisis can have lasting impact.

CUES TO TRUSTWORTHINESS BEFORE THE ENCOUNTER

Before we go on a cruise or meet a surgeon we look to a number of sources for information about the service providers.

Word of Mouth, Ratings, and Blogs

Let's revisit those tourists going to New Zealand for the first time. Customers certainly want some aspects of the encounter to be a surprise. Seeing new sites and meeting new people are the main purpose of tourism. On the other hand, before they make purchase decisions, customers want to know whether the hotels are comfortable, the rooms have good views, the rental car is well maintained and doesn't smell of cigarettes, and seats on the flight over have adequate legroom. But unlike buying a new shirt at Banana Republic, we can't inspect the hotel room or the rental car before embarking on an expensive journey. Instead, we rely on a variety of sources including information provided by the hotels, rental car companies, travel agents, guidebooks, third-party testers like *Consumer Reports*, websites like TripAdvisor and Yelp, and recommendations of friends and families through word of mouth or through Facebook, Twitter, or other social media.

The credibility of the information clearly depends on the source and type of information. Interestingly, vivid descriptions and narratives seem to have a greater impact on customer decisions than statistics or ratings. A story by a neighbor about a positive experience at a hotel is likely to have a stronger influence than the number of stars it got on TripAdvisor. See The Ring of Truth sidebar for a classic study demonstrating the power of vivid stories.[10] One implication is that stories and elaborate comments on websites and social media sites have greater implications for consumer evaluations of trustworthiness than summary scores.

The Ring of Truth

A couple of researchers wondered who students really listen to when they choose their classes. They divided some University of Michigan undergraduates majoring in psychology (you know, the skeptics) into three groups and asked them to list the courses they were likely to enroll in. The first group was the control group, and they were given only the course catalog. The second group got the course catalog and detailed historical data on class enrollment and course evaluations. The third group got the catalog, the historical data, and listened to three students who were enrolled in the classes as they described the courses. The stories embodied in the narratives of the three students demolished the influence of the catalog and the historical data, demonstrating that stories from a few people hold greater sway, even when they run counter to vast statistical summaries. It makes one wonder if they'd have paid such close attention if people their parents' ages had told the stories.

The selection problem is even more complicated for complex professional services (lawyers, surgeons, financial advisors, educators, and such). The most important factor shaping choice would be recommendations from trusted entities, such as friends and relatives, particularly those who possess industry knowledge. Certificates and educational backgrounds of professionals also lend credibility. Think about all those plaques adorning the walls of medical and legal offices. Third-party rating agencies, such as the *U.S. News & World Report* rankings of hospitals and universities, are highly sought after by prospective customers.

Most first-time home buyers struggle to find a good Realtor. Starting out, they probably don't even know the difference between a Realtor (member of the National Association of Realtors) and a real estate agent (someone licensed to sell property). While friends and family members may offer a variety of recommendations, beginners need to focus on what really matters in selecting an agent: experience with properties in their price range, a schedule that fits theirs, willingness to help with other services (like arranging inspections), and patience. Instead, novice home buyers tend to rely on the agent's attire, the office décor, even property prices.

Price and Quality

Although high-quality firms can charge higher prices, for consumers the causation may become inverted as shown in the sidebar "With Placebos, You Get What You Pay For."[11] For consumers high price may connote high quality regardless of whether that is true or false.

With Placebos, You Get What You Pay For

In a shockingly relevant study of pricing, subjects bought energy drinks and then set to work solving puzzles. To the glee of overpriced retailers everywhere, the group that paid the most for the drink actually solved more puzzles than the group that paid less *for the same drink.* The experiment clearly demonstrates that consumers tend to believe that a higher-priced product is better. The shocker lies in the evidence that the product may actually be enhanced by the higher price. We know that the placebo effect works, but now we know you can juice its performance by paying more.

CALCULATED VERSUS BLIND TRUST

So far we have focused on a number of rational and seemingly irrational factors that customers depend on to form their initial opinion of a service provider. We aren't all quite that calculating in every situation. Some relationships—like doctor-patient—elicit something more akin to blind trust. Traditionally, we have maintained a reverence for physicians that places them above questions of competence or motivation. In recent decades, managed care and accelerated research development may have chipped away at the medical pedestal, but unquestioning submission continues to be the norm in large areas of the world.

Calculations of trust are primarily unconscious, of course, and they encompass the sum of our experience. Hence, the lack of information prior to a first encounter does not imply that new customers always come in with high levels of distrust. Since, for the most part, services are delivered as promised, we usually expect the service provider to be trustworthy. A decade ago, when electronic commerce was in its infancy, there was widespread concern about the trustworthiness of websites. Since then, however, the rapid growth of Internet-based retailing has contributed to the demise of many brick-and-mortar retailers, suggesting that we are willing to trust and embrace new providers.

Over the course of a lifetime, experiences and the emotions that accompany them exert a cumulative effect on one's expectations.

Elderly customers sometimes seem unduly skeptical or suspicious, but the provider has no way of knowing how signal events in their lives contribute to their approach to new experiences. In one of our projects we found that older Eastern Europeans lacked confidence in online transactions. Those who demanded a lot of reassurance in their online computer purchase may very well have matured under Soviet rule with its well-known broken promises, privations, and intrusive government. For them, taking a risk with a faceless entity may be a terrifying prospect, whereas it might just seem silly to a gamer or smartphone addict.

CUES TO TRUSTWORTHINESS DURING THE ENCOUNTER

Customers who have been through a particular type of service encounter multiple times have opinions about the trustworthiness of the provider. Their impressions began forming during the first contact and kept developing throughout each iteration of the process. The delivery process itself produced the first opinions, and the emergence of outcomes reinforced (or undermined) them. A wide range of cues feeds into their notions about service employees and the firms they represent, but it all starts with that first impression.

Consider two financial advisors who work for different, but equally reputable, financial institutions. They are competing for a new client, an upper-middle-income professional in his late thirties. Mr. Eagerbeaver wants the potential client to first provide details of his assets and liabilities. Mr. Warmfuzzy gives the client a quick overview of the challenges that come with planning for retirement, the different ways customers approach retirement planning, and the range of services his firm offers. Guess who got the account? The client wasn't about to spill specific details about his private finances before he had taken the measure of the man he would be working with. He couldn't get out of Mr. Eagerbeaver's office fast enough. It is easy to see that despite the strong reputation of a firm's brand, it's crucial that the server or agent first demonstrate personal trustworthiness.

Traditional service management concentrates on familiar behaviors that demonstrate concern for the customer. Service employees are frequently reminded that they are there to serve the customer. But what are the cues that shape perceptions of trust?

Behaviors That Show Interest

It is useful to think of these actions in some sense as service engineering. In Chapter 4 we suggest how several of these can be used as part of a mistake-proofing effort in employee job design.

- **Eye contact.** Nothing delivers a sense of friendly interest more than normal eye contact. Normal because, in some situations, eye contact contributes to a power game, as in noting who blinked first. Liars can often stare right into your face, but suspicion quickly builds for the person who won't look you in the eye.

- **Smiling.** Customers can tell the difference between authentic and inauthentic smiles. Apparently, children as young as six know when a smile is fake. Much work is being conducted these days on enabling computers to identify authentic smiles. We are, however, not very skilled at discovering deceptions and lies.

- **Respect.** Customers can also tell the difference between respect and condescension, respect and obsequiousness, and respect and irony. The alternatives to respect can spoil otherwise productive encounters. Therefore, the most trusted providers have found qualities to admire in the customers and to show their appreciation. Think of Amazon.com with its prominent placement of customer product reviews and Listmania! inventories of customer favorites.

- **Empathy.** Along with recognizing a customer's emotions and appropriately responding, empathy implies a deeper understanding: "I've felt the same way." This kind of response contributes significantly to a sense that the other person really cares. As we see in Chapter 2, analysis of the process flows and transaction history reveals emotions that are most likely to occur during different stages of a service cycle.

- **Assurance.** Once the service provider conveys empathy, the follow-up behavior must convey assurance that feeling the way the customer does is okay. The provider knows what to do and is ready to do it.

- **Effort.** Demonstrating effort shows that the provider is motivated. Consider quotes from two plumbers: one provides details about the work and a breakdown of his costs, and the other gives a single summary quote. The first plumber really thought the job through, made this clear to the customer, and appears to be poised to hit the ground running.

- **Active listening.** By restating the customer's expression, need, or view, servers show that they are really paying attention. The technique ensures that the listener isn't just waiting for an opening to press his or her own agenda.

According to Ms. Agatha Areas, marketing director of Rock in Rio, a firm that organizes rock festivals in Europe and Latin America, Roberto Medina, the CEO, is so obsessed with authenticity that he pays attention to the tiniest details. For one show, he insisted that floral arrangements be placed atop 20-foot-high lampposts, overriding strenuous opposition from frantic bean counters trying to control the expenses. They insisted that no one would notice the arrangements way up there. Medina's string of 10 successes, including the largest music festival in the world, attests to his conviction that this type of attention to detail shapes the customer's trust that the organization is committed to delivering an excellent experience.

Likability Effects

If the need for trust arises from three sources of risk associated with the service provider—know-how, integrity, and availability—then a purely rational judgment of trustworthiness would require us to objectively evaluate each area. But people also pay attention to their feelings when making judgments; they talk about listening to their gut or "that little voice inside." How we feel about a service provider or a service firm affects our trust. If we like people, we tend to believe that they're going to want to help us. This is largely because we want to think they like us back. But, really, likability is the product of a wide range of qualities that may have no bearing whatsoever on risk, including appearance, gender, ethnicity, wit, cheerfulness, compassion, and warmth. At the same time, people don't want to take a risk with someone they don't like, and customers don't like providers who seem cold, domineering, unsocial, overconfident, gloomy, impolite, phony, or discourteous.[12]

Appearing Competent

Knowing much less than the provider does about the service puts customers at a disadvantage when it comes to judging competence. Credibility and evidence of prior accomplishments dominate the assessment, but we also rate professional competence according to body language and the provider's ability to explain relevant issues clearly rather than take refuge in jargon. Body language refers to nonverbal cues that can reinforce or undermine the verbal content. Erect posture and confident hand gestures make people appear competent and elicit trustworthiness.

Explanations

As for ability and willingness to explain matters clearly, healthcare providers struggle to impart essential information and elicit compliance in matters that can mean the difference between life and death. A major health insurer based in Michigan provides nursing support to chronically ill patients.[13] Every two weeks, a nurse calls these patients to inquire about their health and to provide guidance and support as needed. The following excerpts are taken from two actual conversations:

Conversation 1

Nurse Amy: Do you see the dentist every six months?

Patient: Yes.

Nurse Amy: Good. Do you know the relationship between your teeth and heart?

Patient: No. I have never heard of anything.

Nurse Amy: If you get a gum infection and it is not taken care of, then you can get an infection in your bloodstream. Your heart is the main pump of the blood, and sometimes you can develop infections around your heart. It doesn't happen all the time. But things like endocarditis, which is the infection of the area around the heart, can happen.

Patient: Ooh, . . .

Conversation 2

Nurse Clara: Do you see the dentist every six months?

Patient: No.

Nurse Clara: You should see one regularly.

Patient: Why?

Nurse Clara: It prevents infections.

Patient: Oh.

In this study an experimental group received guidelines to restructure the call along a number of principles articulated in this book. One of the guidelines was to offer clear explanations. The control group continued old practices. The experimental group was perceived to be more competent relative to the control group.

Decision Rules

Compelling evidence indicates that customers generally follow simple rules to make selections. People just don't develop normative models that require them to identify and quantify the trade-offs involved in choosing one item over another. In financial services, the classic trade-off is between risk and return, and yet, even professors of finance are known to follow naive rules for investing their retirement funds. Despite the fact that customers may be overwhelmed by rational decision models, they do expect competent professionals to articulate the trade-offs and utilize sophisticated decision tools to optimize them.[14]

The risk of opportunistic behavior is rooted in integrity, and the risk of incompetence is an issue of skill and knowledge. Customers muddle them, however, letting their perception of a provider's integrity or benevolence affect their assessment of competence. It may be as simple as jumping to the conclusion that a caring provider who truly understands what a client needs ("He gets it.") must be competent. But just because he gets your problem, doesn't mean that he grasps all the technical issues involved or has the resources or skill to resolve it.

Servicescapes

Service providers have long employed a number of familiar factors that seem even less rational to influence our judgments of trustworthiness. Firms know that the service provider's store, office, website, clinic, or restaurant affects the emotions and behaviors of customers and employees, an idea that Joie de Vivre Hospitality has put to good use with its 28 themed hotels. Where trust is an issue, providers work hard to make the *servicescapes*, locations where the service encounter occurs, all but reek of credibility by selecting the color, lighting, grandeur, tone, sound, and even chocolates on the counter to convey the desired impression. The physical appearance of the professionals and their adherence to professional norms also shape perceptions of trustworthiness.[15] If the servicescape is in cyberspace, the provider carefully selects layout, colors, and wording for the website.[16] None of it actually proves trustworthiness, but it plays into the customer's limited ability to select cues that really matter. If a lawyer's secretary makes scheduling errors or her servicescape (office) is messy, our estimation of the attorney's competence may suffer.[17]

Dress to Impress

Shakaib Rehman and coauthors surveyed 400 patients of an average age of 53 regarding their preferences for physician attire. They found a strong preference for physicians dressed in a white coat. Patients intimated greater confidence in and were more willing to share their personal problems with physicians who were professionally dressed. How female physicians were dressed appeared to matter more than how their male counterparts were dressed.

BUILDING YOUR TRUST FUND

There are a number of actions service providers can undertake to ensure that customers accurately assess trustworthiness.

Do It Right the First Time and Every Time

There is absolutely no substitute for a positive outcome. We cannot overemphasize the importance of error elimination tools like poka-yokes (see Chapter 5, "Control") and process-improvement disciplines, such as Six Sigma, lean, and total quality management (TQM) programs that eliminate errors and ensure processes deliver the desired outcomes. Of course, we're assuming that the firm is geared to deliver what the customer wants.

Insulate Your Customer from Risk

Firms can diminish some of the risks that customer are exposed to. This can be done through service guarantees. Risk can also be reduced through performance evaluation measures that align the employees' interests with those of the customer, making the customer aware of this alignment. AAA tow truck operations in Los Angeles does this well. Operators inform the customers that they will be surveyed and that their satisfaction scores will have a bearing on the operator.

Your Satisfaction Guaranteed

As a visiting professor at the Harvard Business School, I (Chase) had an office next to Chris Hart, who had just published a widely read article on the power of unconditional service guarantees.[18] It described specific assurances that Domino's Pizza, Federal Express, Hampton Inns, and L.L.Bean built right into the service encounter. Hart claimed in the article that guarantees functionally eliminated the risk customers took to try the products. On my return to USC, I wondered, "What if I offered a satisfaction guarantee to potential students of my service operations elective?" After all, taking a class consumes students' time and resources.

So I sent a memo to all USC MBA students, describing the course and my guarantee, which was to pay for their books, cases, and $500 toward the course fee if they were not satisfied with the class. I included two caveats: they had to let me know in advance if the class wasn't going well, and they could not wait and decide whether or not they liked the grade, first, before they took me up on it. They could, however, collect after the grades were in. The result: enrollment jumped from 25 students the year before to 82. A reporter covered my story for the *Wall Street Journal*, and I appeared on television to discuss it. Not one student collected, by the way. The guarantee signaled my motivation and competence to deliver the teaching service, thus certifying my trustworthiness.

Proactively Identify and Prevent Vulnerabilities

Educate the customer about any risks or actions that may create vulnerabilities. Verizon texts customers to warn them when they are about to exceed the data limit for their plans, which may create additional fees. The customers learn about the risk far enough in advance that they have time to take corrective action. Progressive, the insurance company represented in ads by the exceedingly chipper Flo dressed in white, heads off customer speculation as to possible better prices elsewhere by displaying competitor policy rates on its own website. Truly concerned customers would probably double-check the prices, anyway, but Progressive comes off as especially forthright.

Inform Your Customer About the Risks and Problems

Make customers aware of potential problems. Installers of DirecTV satellite dishes are required to tell homeowners that an extra charge may apply if the distance from the antenna to the controller in the living room exceeds a certain length, though it seldom does. In healthcare, the informed consent and waiver paperwork that must be signed prior to a medical procedure enumerates the risks to the patient, but the true goal is to insulate the provider from risks. Nevertheless, surgeons frequently reassure their patients that they will do their best to ensure that everything will go well. In the world of hospitality, this translates into being up front when the hotel is especially busy and the room assignment is not going to be as nice as expected. The worst thing the desk clerk can do is withhold the explanation about the room and disingenuously upsell another service.

Listen to Your Customer

In face-to-face interactions, active listening is a critical skill that conveys that the customer matters and helps the service provider discover what the customer needs. Leading providers of complex professional services dedicate the initial interaction to learning about the customers and finding out how their service fits into the customers' lives. At Cedars-Sinai Medical Center in Los Angeles, radiation oncologist Michele Burnisom uses the first few sessions to learn about her patients. What is the family situation? What information do they want and how much information can they emotionally handle? How does the patient prefer to make decisions? Similarly, Brenda, the early childhood specialist, spends several hours with her clients—parents struggling to process their child's diagnosis—early on to understand the anxieties, concerns, and family dynamics.

Track Your Encounters

Web and telephone interactions, on the other hand, are mechanical and make it hard to develop relationships with customers. Instead of counting on one or two frontline employees, as was the case decades ago, companies use information compiled about the customer to give transactions the personal touch. Either customer service reps access the data, or customers themselves encounter it on the company website. Amazon.com uses a data mining technique called *market basket analysis* to make it easy for customers to review their past purchases and evaluate other products that they might be interested in. Further advance in meaningful personalization of this nature can only help build relationships.

Tracking transaction histories across multiple contact points is as important as tracking purchase information. Most of us can recall interactions with call centers where we've had to restate the same problem again and again to different agents. Lack of familiarity with prior interactions, particularly those that have gone poorly, infuriates customers, who see it as a sign of disrespect and incompetence. Tracking all transactions also allows companies to remind customers about transactions that went well, which acts as an advertisement while building goodwill.

Tracking data and other information pertinent to the entire encounter is also essential to employees who manage the customer experience face-to-face. Does the nurse know about the visits the patient made to the emergency room prior to being admitted today? Does the airline agent checking in the passengers know the configuration of the aircraft? Does the hotel front desk understand the encounter routines of business customers?

Align Employee Traits with Your Customers' Information Needs

Savvy service providers know their market and know which segments need to be assured that the products are right for them. They make sure that the website contains employee photos and images of situations and cultures that project the firm's interest and knowledge about customer needs. A large Internet PC purveyor learned this the hard way, having employed images of young customers to invigorate the brand. Since many of their first-time buyers were older individuals, anxiety about picking the right retailer resulted in numerous phone calls seeking assurance about their transactions.

Perceived similarity also improves communication and enhances motivation.[19] Compliance with the Weight Watchers program is highest when clients perceive the representatives as similar to themselves. Perceived cultural similarity can also quickly allay customer concerns about provider comprehension and sympathies. Swarovski's Crystal Worlds receives visitors from 60 countries, and they have employees from 28 countries.

Adhere to Norms and Rituals

While similarity in culture or attitude is valuable when customers are unsure whether a solution is appropriate for them, similarity is less valuable when customers are concerned about the service provider's ability (competence, resources, availability) to deliver a known solution. In this case, sticking to industry norms in dress code, process steps, décor, and so on, is more reassuring.

Demonstrate Knowledge About Your Customer

Familiarity breeds liking; liking promotes relationships; and relationships build trust. A physician who remembers the name of her patient's daughter implies something more than a perfunctory clinical interest in the patient. Databases, CRMs, and affinity analysis applications make it easy for firms to track preferences and details about prior interactions and to individually tailor services. Thus personalization demonstrates interest in the customer as an individual and increases costs to the customer of switching providers. One does need to exercise a degree of caution in using transaction history information in ways that may seem from the provider's standpoint to be a win-win for both parties. Leveraging this knowledge to reach deeper into the customer wallet while providing more targeted service can raise privacy concerns—in which case the trust bank balance would go to zero.

Show Your Effort

It pays to show customers that you are working for their business. A motivated Realtor really listens to the eager house hunters and shows up the next day with a handful of carefully selected properties. On the other hand, if the house hunters show up for an appointment at the office before the Realtor arrives, the entire firm will seem unmotivated and indifferent unless idle staff members step up and keep them productively occupied.

Back to the case of that big PC company that was deluged with phone calls from first-time buyers. It was 2006, and the calls were coming from Eastern Europe. These customers had no prior experience buying high-value products online and were just calling to confirm that their orders were being processed and to track the status. In the absence of an order-tracking system, the firm was losing money in dealing with phone calls from untrusting customers checking on budget products with small profit margins. If those worried European novices could have simply checked their orders online as many times a day as they wished, they could have taken comfort in knowing that their PCs hadn't been lost and they hadn't been forgotten. They would have observed that their order was steadily progressing through the supply chain. In fact, it's become a part of the fun of ordering from Amazon.com (or Zappos, Overstock, Tiger Direct, NewEgg, etc.)

to follow the tracking link and find out which warehouse just scanned your package along its journey to your residence.

"Cannot" Is Better Than "Will Not"

We'll be saying more than once that "cannot" is better than "will not." An overwhelming majority of customers are reasonable and recognize legitimate constraints faced by organizations. Customers have a sense of what should be done, but they may not know what can be done. Even in extremely challenging situations, such as a case in which a child was burned in an accident and the 911 operator told the frantic parent that an ambulance couldn't be dispatched because the situation wasn't life threatening, a clear explanation dispelled the parent's anger.[20] On the other hand, when service providers merely assert that they won't act, customers perceive a cold, personal affront rather than a systematic decision.

The Arizona Diamondbacks have leveraged this concept into a program called "Find a Way to Say Yes." Diamondbacks fans know about the program, and they expect the employees to respond in this way to their requests. Of course, not all requests can be met as stated. Derrick Hall, CEO and president of the Diamondbacks, finesses this challenge daily. For example, when fans find good seats at the ballpark that are empty, they want to know if they can have them. Ushers are instructed to point out the possibility that the ticket holders may eventually come to the game, but if the seats are available by the seventh inning, then the fans can have them.

How to Refuse Celebrities

Hotelier Ali Kasikci has managed exclusive luxury hotels all over the world, so he's heard every impossible request a well-heeled (i.e., spoiled) client can make. Some years ago, when he was managing The Peninsula Beverly Hills, two celebrity guests always sought the same suite. Luckily, their visits didn't coincide for years, and Kasikci maintained two very happy customers. But, then it happened. He learned that they were both going to arrive on the same weekend. Rather than refuse one of them, he elected to refuse both! He had the suite under contention draped with plastic construction material and said that it had been closed for renovation on those dates. He apologized for being unable to give them their room despite his best intentions. It was far better to lose the fee than the customers.

Make Sure Controllable Elements Are Error-Free

When customers cannot judge the true skills of a service provider, they use all other aspects of the business to form impressions. Did the sheet rocker tidy up? Is the office clean? Is the Realtor tracking phone calls from potential buyers and responding promptly?

Explain and Don't Use Jargon

Sprinkling conversation with geeky technical terms puts people off and confuses the issues. When a lower-ranking member of the technical staff uses the terms, rather than the boss or high-end professional, they can appear pretentious instead of knowledgeable. Providing information that is understandable to the ordinary mortal customer is the key to demonstrating capability.

Don't Exploit Vulnerability

In the movie *Miracle on 34th Street*, the department store Santa Claus at Macy's suggests that a customer "Go to Gimbel's" for a certain product. The advice made the customer loyal to Macy's for life, because it showed the staff to be dedicated to solving the customer's problem rather than making a sale for Macy's at all costs. This reflects a basic tenet of trust: when a relatively dependent party trusts the dominant partner's honesty and benevolence, the dependent party's fear of exploitation and the resultant feelings of uncertainty decline.[21] Customers avidly recommend Ken's Automotive Shop in the San Fernando Valley because each has experienced situations in which Ken refused to charge or charged some token amount for a problem requiring minimal effort.

Celebrate Success and Exploit Social Networking

Inform the customer of your success stories. Announce such data as number of on-time deliveries and percentage of patients who have fully recovered after knee surgery. Remember that stories and narratives from trusted sources are more powerful then summary statistics. It pays to proactively manage social networks, and events that celebrate success are even more powerful. People flock to the big parade held for every sports team that wins a championship. When the Minnesota Twins won the World Series in 1987, practically the whole state flocked to St. Paul to watch the parade in the freezing cold. The event is legendary. And even when the Los Angeles Lakers win yet another of their many NBA championships, hundreds of thousands of people line the parade route to reaffirm the team's mythic status in the sports world.

KEY PRINCIPLES FOR BUILDING TRUST

Trust plays a crucial role in how a service encounter is processed. Lack of trust can increase customer anxiety and render the experience unpleasant for the provider and the customer. Below we list a set of principles that firms can employ to enhance trust.

1. *Really* **listen to customers.** This is very hard to do, especially if you have employees who really know their stuff. Consultants, for example, by their nature are usually way ahead of their clients and force fit the problem and solution strategy plans into their own models and constructs. This kind of overreach,

when discovered by the client, can destroy the nascent "trust fund" being built by the consultant.

2. **Inform the customer about the risks and problems.** This is where honesty becomes the most powerful trust-building approach of all.

3. **Don't exploit vulnerability.** You probably don't need any business ethics statements other than this.

4. **Demonstrate effort.** Trying hard is a weak substitute for competence, but other things being equal, it is a great tiebreaker when choosing among service providers.

4

SHAPING YOUR CUSTOMERS' PERCEPTIONS OF CONTROL

Have it your way.

—Excerpt from a Burger King jingle
from the 1980s

A key factor underlying our perceptions of service encounters is the degree to which we believe we control the experience. To function effectively, however, service providers need to control encounters. Through the clever application of psychology and process design, providers can manage customer actions (*behavioral control*) before, during, and after the encounter and yet make the system behind the encounter sufficiently transparent so that the customer knows that it's well managed (*cognitive control*) and continues to feel personally autonomous. Success at this delicate maneuvering depends on the service provider's ability to develop efficient and unobtrusive strategies for persuading customers to surrender control over some aspects of the transaction.

CONTROL MATTERS

We humans need to believe that we control our destiny and that our efforts make things turn out the way we want. We abhor the idea that we're subject to outside forces. After all, when people commit crimes, we imprison them and thereby minimize the control they have over their activities. We also have a difficult time believing that outcomes are influenced by random events. We work to maintain what psychologists call the *illusion of control*. People are fooling themselves, of course, if they think it helps to blow on dice before rolling them, select stock based on a "gut feeling," or wear the same dirty socks to keep a hitting streak alive. On the surface, it's just superstition, intellectual laziness, or the desire to maintain one's self-esteem as exemplified by the bravado-laden refrain "You're not the boss of me now" from the theme to the old TV show *Malcolm in the Middle*.

Although that's certainly true to some extent, we have an even stronger need to believe that we are playing on a level field in a predictable world where we can bend circumstances to our will. Think back to childhood and the conviction that you could control the direction of the kiddy car at the amusement park even though

Table 4.1 We want control and choice when . . .

We paid for it.	"Since I'm a first-class passenger, I want you to serve me my meal at 7 p.m. Pacific time."
Creature comfort is involved.	"Anywhere but the middle seat on the plane."
Time is a factor.	Instructions to the taxi driver for beating the cross-town traffic from Santa Monica to Hollywood: "Stay off Wilshire. Take Fountain Avenue instead."
Health and safety are the issue.	"Who is the best orthopedist for knee replacements?"

it was mounted on a rail. Even as adults, we operate under the illusion that repeatedly pressing the button at a crosswalk makes the light change sooner when in fact traffic engineers completely disable the switches at some intersections during peak traffic periods.

When we enjoy a sense of control, we feel free and relaxed. Mills and Krantz allowed one group of blood donors to choose the arm from which blood was collected while another group was not given this choice. The group that had control concerning which arm the blood would be drawn from reported less pain.[1] Loss of control can result in stress, anxiety, and in some cases anger.

In the world of services, our desire for control and its companion, choice, may encompass a wide range of attributes, but it invariably includes economic ones. See Table 4.1 for examples.

COMPONENTS OF CONTROL: BEHAVIORAL AND COGNITIVE CONTROL

We think we have control over a service encounter when we perceive that we have choice, influence, and cognitive control. We have a choice when we can select the desired service product, such as the restaurant to go to for dinner or a specific dish off the menu. Influence is the power we sense ourselves exerting over the service process, such as inducing our waiter at the restaurant to be particularly atten-tive. Influence includes the ability to control our own actions and manage our creature comforts, such as freedom to move around the plane during a flight. These are all examples of behavioral control.

Cognitive control is the perception that events are predictable, derived from having witnessed enough of the system behind the ser-vice encounter that we trust it. Thus while we don't really control the service process, our experience with the system leads us to believe that things are "in control." For example, experience tells us that we will be processed in order of arrival at the bank or answered in turn on a helpline, which gives us a feeling of control.

MOMENTS THAT INFLUENCE YOUR CUSTOMERS' PERCEPTION OF CONTROL

When major events derail plans or reorganize our lives, the sensa-tion is that of spinning out of control. Dazed faces reveal disorien-tation and confusion when the doctor has bad news or the driver steps out of his damaged car after a chain-reaction collision. Feeling flummoxed by a prolonged slide in the stock market, impending retirement, or even the prospect of a new baby is the first of a range of complex feelings. People confronting a loss of control may go on to display joy, impatience, depression, fear, anger, anxiety, or even exhilaration, all of which they may well share with the poor service representative trying to help them.

The prospect of losing control can be so painful that we go to great lengths to allay, avoid, or deny it. The more information we gather about the layout, culture, transportation system, restaurants, and entertainment options in a city we've never visited, the more comfortable we feel about going there. The same is true about buy-ing a laptop for the first time: preparation engenders a sense of con-trol over events. Avoidance postpones the loss of control.

Denial creates a distorted sense of cognitive control. It can mani-fest itself as slickly as when pundits ignore the statisticians during elections but eventually make fools of themselves on television. It can include "sour grapes" statements like, "I didn't really want that client, anyway," rather than face the reality of rejection. It even extends to elaborate efforts at cognitive reinterpretation—construing events in such a way as to make them seem fair. If two diners complain in the same night that their food arrived cold, the restaurateur who responds by saying, "Good! They weren't the sort of customer I want," is not likely to develop a large, devoted following.

BATTLES FOR CONTROL

It will come as no surprise, then, that the customer is only one of several parties feeling a need for control. In service encounters, the struggle actually involves battles between each of the participants: customer, server, and service firm. The multiple permutations of the struggle are collectively known as a "three-cornered fight" (see Figure 4.1).[2]

Service Firm Versus Server

This conflict pits the firm's goal to contain costs against the servers' drive to exercise some control over their work environment.

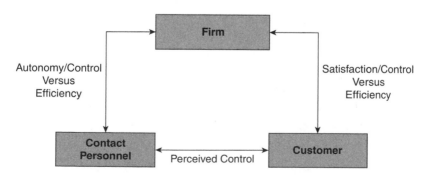

Figure 4.1 The three-way battle for control

Source: John E. G. Bateson, *Managing Services Marketing* (New York: Dryden HBJ, 1991), p. 98.

Delegating a degree of autonomy and control to employees empowers them to deal with unforeseen situations, but it comes at the price of higher recruiting and training costs and higher salaries. The desire to minimize these costs impels the firm to impose greater control over a cheaper but less capable workforce with reduced discretionary authority to handle the full range of customer service issues.

Customer Versus Service Firm

The conflict between the customer and the firm derives from the customer's desire for the satisfaction that comes from exercising more freedom—"Have it your way"—and the firm's resistance to the inherent inefficiencies created by allowing flexibility. *Seinfeld*'s soup Nazi exemplifies extreme control, but a visit to the Internet turns up dozens of disgruntled posts by consumers complaining about the gourmet restaurant that wouldn't substitute a glass of white wine for the red on the *prix fixe* menu, the high-end hotel that charged the guest for a room when weather delayed the flight, the airline that makes it nearly impossible to use frequent flyer miles. At the other end of the continuum lies the busy golf course that allows golfers to slow play (i.e., linger at each hole), the hotel that lets guests stay past checkout time even when arriving guests need access to the room, or the Internet service provider (ISP) that installs communications hardware but ends up troubleshooting the customer's ink-jet printer.

Server Versus Customer

The nature of the conflict between service employee and customer in everyday service encounters is well known to us all. Blame sometimes rests on the penny-pinching firm that maintains an incompetent workforce. Fundamentally, however, the conflict arises from the role of the service employee as gatekeeper who is charged with enforcing company policy. In contrast to the cases of excessive flexibility cited above, golf course marshals press dawdling players to pick up their balls and proceed to the next hole, hotel desk clerks remind lingering guests to vacate the room, and the ISP technician offers to arrange additional service at an additional charge. Not to be lost here is the desire by other customers to see visible evidence of order being maintained. Visits to other cultures can illuminate the struggle for control, as demonstrated by the "traveler's check incident."

Traveler's Check Incident

Back in the day, your hapless gringo author, Dick, took a trip to Mexico with his family. Needing to cash a traveler's check in Guadalajara before returning home, he wandered into a neighborhood bank dressed in the travel gear of the 1970s—Bermuda shorts and a Hawaiian shirt, and he was wearing several cameras around his neck. He was directed to a manager's desk where he endorsed the check. Then he was sent to a teller counter at the far end of the room, which was surrounded by a dozen people trying to make transactions. As he waited among the customers, Dick saw that he was not making progress because customers arriving *after* him were moving to the window. After waiting for some time, he recrossed the lobby to the manager's desk and pleaded in very broken Spanish, saying that he had one day to see this beautiful city and could the manager help him with changing the money. "Lo siento," replied the manager, shaking his head and pointing back at the teller, "No se puedo ayudar."

Dejected, Dick shuffled back across the lobby, when, lo and behold, the mob split in two, creating an aisle down which Dick walked directly to the front of the line where the teller promptly served him. Apparently, word of his plight had traveled through the bank, and locals bent the rules for the ignorant American. He never did learn the rules for waiting his turn at banks in Mexico.

Server Versus Server, the Occasional Fourth Corner

Competition exists in the workplace as it does everywhere else, and the battle for control can transpire between employees within the service system. A story dredged from the annals of 1960s psychology apocrypha (Elias Porter probably made it up)[3] claims that it used to be common practice for waiters to tell chefs what to cook first, but that chefs resented the custom, interpreting it as taking commands from lower-status employees. In the style of all good parables, a wise but lowly person ultimately hit upon the idea of a metal spindle with clips for attaching order slips. Placed in the window of the serving counter, the spindle became the interface between waiter and chef. The chef could quickly see the orders as they came in and choose what to cook first. The so-called parable of the spindle is often presented to illustrate how technologies that different employees use in different ways can reduce tension by accommodating status differences.

ALLOCATING CONTROL TO YOUR CUSTOMER THROUGH CHOICE

Firms cede control to customers whenever they give them the option of choosing. As we discussed above, some choices are easy for the customer to make and cost the firm nothing. A number of airlines now have a bar in the economy section that has water, fruit juices, and snacks. Passengers can serve themselves whenever they want. While the bar frees up the cabin crew's time, its main psychological benefit is one of increasing a sense of control for passengers. They can get a drink when they want and stretch their legs. The airline reduces the workload on its staff, and at the same time it improves customers' experience.

A challenge facing many sports teams in the United States is to attract fans to watch the game at the stadium. The quality of television broadcasting and the hassles of going to the stadium are making it more attractive to stay at home. One approach for combating this trend is to provide more options at the stadium. The Arizona Diamondbacks are developing technologies that allow visitors at the stadium to access a number of different camera feeds on their smartphones. Visitors can select the camera angle they prefer while watching the replay.

Unfortunately not all choices are easy for the customer to make and as a result they would prefer not to choose. In return for surrendering autonomy and accepting dependency, customers expect peace of mind. Two factors leading to dependency are the scary realization that with control comes responsibility for the outcome and the crushing conviction that there are too many options. Many people would rather let someone else make a tough decision. In the absence of clear evidence about the value of different treatments for breast cancer, for instance, the person who makes the choice must accept accountability for any negative outcome resulting from the selection. Many people also find themselves more averse to some areas of decision making than others. A good example is personal finance, particularly investing.

An idea that enjoyed brief popularity in 2005 was put forth by President Bush in a State of the Union address wherein he proposed partially privatizing social security. Under his plan, workers could steer a portion of their payroll tax contribution into a private investment account that they would manage for their future retirement. Besides opposition to undercutting the social security trust fund, many Americans panicked at the idea that they would now need to develop investment expertise on top of their other responsibilities. "I might as well throw my money away at the blackjack tables," declared a friend to whom the stock market looks like a horror show of games and caprice run by a nasty cabal.

Struck by the response to President Bush's proposal, professors Simona Botti at Cornell and Sheena Iyengar at Columbia compiled data from multiple studies regarding personal choice. They found that public policies maximizing choice, "which is seemingly desirable and beneficial, can become paralyzing and debilitating." Even when the issue is as ordinary as selecting jam, respondents make a purchase much more often when the choices are limited rather than when there are dozens of options. This tendency to avoid choosing extends to important issues as well. Having too many choices—even with the assurance that the options are good ones—is associated with reduced satisfaction and inflated payment for the final selection. Increasing the complexity of the choices makes matters even worse.

Getting people to take responsibility for their retirement savings didn't get any easier after the 2008 economic meltdown called attention to the amount of real risk involved. Even before the collateralized debt obligation (CDO) bubble burst, though, behavioral economists struggled to create strategies for getting Americans to enroll in a 401(k) or some other *defined contribution retirement plan*. The *defined benefit plan*, a.k.a. pension, was going the way of the dodo as employers off-loaded most of the cost. The responsibility of saving for retirement has shifted to the employees. Although some employers are contributing to defined contribution plans by matching a portion of the employee's contribution, the employees bear all the risk. However, 401(k) plans have their charms: they're portable from one job to the next, they're taxed only when the owner makes a withdrawal, and employees control their own funds. Unfortunately, half the workers in the private sector don't have access to a 401(k), only two-thirds of those who do actually participate, and most of them save too little and invest it ignorantly. Each of these issues involves choice, and some involve many choices. Financial service providers clearly need to step up their game.

Financial education at the workplace and online tools to help employees evaluate their needs and preferences help a little. Some plan sponsors eliminate choice altogether by automating assignment and balance based on participant characteristics. An increasingly popular system called Save More Tomorrow, devised by economist Shlomo Benartzi, depicts the "hurt" in future terms by having participants commit to automatically increasing their contribution with every pay raise, so they never see the gross amount on the check shrink. Various versions of the plan also minimize the number of choices by offering a limited number of portfolios based on risk tolerance or target maturity dates.

Service providers need to appreciate laypeople's stress when they are confronted by complex decisions affecting their own well-being and that of the persons they cherish. To experts, having many choices in their field seems like an array of doors to opportunity. To anyone outside that field, especially when the ramifications are potentially life-changing, the situation may seem more like choosing a door in *The Lady or the Tiger*.

ALLOCATING CONTROL TO YOUR CUSTOMER THROUGH SELF-SERVICE

The level of control customers have on the service they receive can also be increased by increasing their involvement in the production of the service. This gives them the freedom to decide how they want the service done—the salad bar model of service delivery. The current trend of incorporating juice bars in the main cabin of aircrafts illustrates the control benefits of self-service. Shouldice Hospital based in the outskirts of Toronto, Canada, specializes in hernia surgery. This hospital was one of the first hospitals to encourage patients to walk almost immediately after surgery instead of being pushed around in a wheelchair. This "self-service" accelerated recovery and increased patients' control over their daily activities.[4] The Internet creates abundant opportunities for firms to delegate control to customers. An extreme example of this is the firm eBay. All the activities are performed by the customers; eBay provides a software platform that enables transactions and acts as a trusted intermediary.

Most service work entails some degree of participation on the part of the customer. Participation can take place inside or outside the service facility, and it can be described as active or passive, as

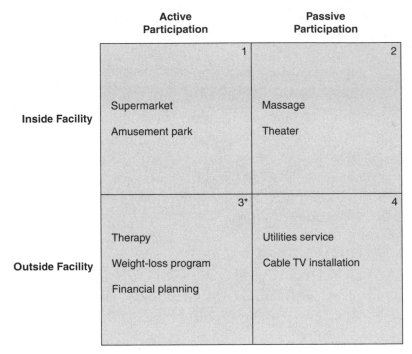

Figure 4.2 Classification of customer participation in services

*Compliance dependent services (CDS)
Source: Stephanie Dellande and Mary C. Gilly, "Gaining Customer Compliance in Services,"
Advances in Services Marketing and Management 7, 274–292.

shown in Figure 4.2. In quadrant 1, which addresses active participation, the customer inside the supermarket has to participate actively by selecting food and taking it to the checkout counter. Inside an amusement park, customer enjoyment is enhanced by customers being actively involved in the experience. Participation in quadrant 2 is primarily passive, involving only occasional verbal feedback about the massage to the masseur or applauding the actors' performance in the theater, both of which are manifestations of control. Likewise, participation in quadrant 4 is passive except for the rare occasion when things go wrong and the customer must help troubleshoot the problem in order to fix it. "Troubleshooting a TV Problem" illustrates a creative way to control customer actions while preserving their self-esteem.

Troubleshooting a TV Problem

When cable television companies troubleshoot problems over the telephone, the most common problem they encounter involves reception. Often, customers have inadvertently changed the channel setting on the TV set. When a service rep asks the customer if the TV is "on the correct channel," the customer, perhaps feeling embarrassed, will often automatically say yes. A quick troubleshooting routine employed by one company gets around the issue by first instructing the customer to turn the channel selector to channel 5. Next, the server says to select channel 3 (the correct channel). This process circumvents customer embarrassment and ensures that the check is performed methodically.

The conditions in quadrant 3 tend to be the most complicated because customers perform much of the actual service on their own time, outside the supervision of the service provider. Though the provider directs customers in the application of the service, the provider relinquishes control early in the process, and the customer decides whether, or to what extent, to comply. Ultimately, the customer determines the service outcome.

Such *client-dependent services* have been studied extensively by marketing expert Stephanie Dellande.[5] Focusing on the role of the service provider in achieving customer compliance, she analyzed performance at a weight-loss clinic and found that both the expertise and similarity of the provider to clients in terms of demographics, beliefs, and values elicited the client attributes necessary for compliance, which are role clarity, ability, and motivation. Customers who were clear about what they had to do, had the ability to do it, and were motivated to follow through were more likely to be successful in weight reduction. Professionals who were experts in the field of weight control were able to explain customer roles clearly and could demonstrate appropriate behavior. Similar demographic character-istics, beliefs, and values emerged as important because customers who perceived that they were similar to their weight-loss counselors were more inclined to understand the directions they were given and more motivated to perform their weight-loss tasks.

As with choice, there is a limit to what a customer can do or is willing to do. Some customers would simply prefer the firm or the service provider to get things done.

FRAMEWORK FOR SHARING CONTROL WITH YOUR CUSTOMERS

The battle breakdown suggests that the ongoing question for profes-sional service firms is determining who should call the shots con-cerning what activities the customers should perform. Although the organization's strategy determines the general locus of control, the more practical question is how decisions and tasks are delegated. Though one might think that customers should make decisions for themselves, they can do that responsibly and with a reasonable chance of success only if they fully understand the options and the consequences. The service provider may have the deeper under-standing and better skills but requires the customer's consent, none-theless. Figure 4.3 illustrates the nature of the trade-offs from the customer's perspective.

Dependency

Customer willingness to relinquish control increases with the complexity of the information required and the significance of the decision, as illustrated by the block in the upper right corner of Figure 4.3. Hospital patients readily cede control to the surgeon for decisions requiring professional medical knowledge. When it comes to knee replacements, for example, more than 150 different prosthetic devices are available. Orthopedists prefer to implant the model with

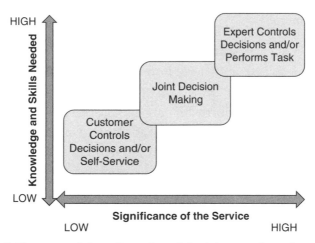

Figure 4.3 Framework for allocation of decisions and service activities

which they have the most experience for the type of joint damage presented, while patients often know very little about different prosthetic options. During the surgery, even if patients generally remained conscious, they could hardly be expected to weigh in on discoveries made in the course of the procedure. Hence, the patient accepts a temporary state of total dependency, placing trust in the surgeon and exchanging autonomy for a sense of security. Of course, the surgeon anticipates the possibility of uncontrollable outcomes and obtains the patient's consent and a waiver of liability before even beginning a procedure.

Preference

On the other hand, many decision-making opportunities arise in the course of a hospital stay for which patients are adequately informed and the results of which are by and large psychological in nature. Where the continuums of complexity and significance meet, we enter the realm of preference, as shown in the block on the bottom left of Figure 4.3. Service providers do well to relinquish control to the customer in such cases. Thus, hospitals make it a point to let patients choose their meals, control the lighting in their rooms, and, for the most part, entertain visitors whenever they feel up to it.

Shared Control

Sometimes, in cases where a certain degree of knowledge is necessary and the consequences are important but not dire, control can be successfully shared by the service provider and the customer. Under these circumstances, the service provider must balance the consequence (cost) of relinquishing total control (dependency) against the benefits of the customer shouldering responsibility (autonomy) for the consequence (outcome) by taking some control. Thus the apparent cost to the service provider produces a benefit in the form of shared responsibility. In healthcare, improved compliance, better outcomes, and reduced costs have been associated with the move from the physician making all the treatment decisions to shared decision making between physician and patient.[6] In the case of the surgical patient, the physician may need to spend some time listening to the patient's priorities, preferences, and goals and then supply information as to pain management, therapy, and recovery options.

The distinction between preference and knowledge and the dangers inherent in misinterpretation should be obvious. Even in the most mundane service interactions, customers are known to let their desires blind them to the difference. Wishful thinking is common in impulse purchases where the deal truly is too good to be true, placing the blame for the errant purchase on a lapse of due diligence on the part of the purchaser rather than false claims on the part of the seller.

Buyer Beware

We got an earful at the office about an incident involving our colleague, Mendy, who inherited a 1966 Ford Mustang and decided to sell it. He hired Tony the detailer to come to his house to clean the car in preparation for an upcoming classic car show and sale. Tony asked if he wanted the engine steam-cleaned. Mendy thought a spotless engine sounded good and told him to go ahead. After Tony finished the job and returned to his home 20 miles away, Mendy discovered to his chagrin that moisture from the steam cleaning had shorted out the wiring in the ancient starter. The car wouldn't start. More than a little upset, he called Tony, described the problem, and demanded to know why he wasn't warned. After all, Mendy had emphasized at the outset that he knew nothing about cars, so he assumed that Tony would have mentioned the likelihood that decades of oil and grease had corroded the plastic coating on the wires. Tony insisted that he'd merely asked Mendy if he wanted it steam-cleaned, and Mendy had said yes, so that was his assignment—no further questions. The moral of the story: be careful not to confuse preference with knowledge, and, certainly, never hire Tony the detailer!

Many niche experts base their value proposition on moving customers from preference, where little appears to be at stake, to dependence, where decisions are critical and complex. Such a transaction requires customers to shift their trust and exchange considerable autonomy for an enhanced sense of security, and perhaps to even change allegiances. For instance, say an external consultant convinces company management that the consequences of a proposed study of the corporate IT infrastructure are more significant than they thought. Then, suppose that the consultant demonstrates knowledge and skill superior to that of the in-house group, which the managers had assumed would perform the study. That hypothetical consultant is now in great shape to close the deal and perform the study. Said consultant should also be prepared to market additional services if the study indicates that alterations or upgrades are needed.

Ultimately, the dominant party in the battle for control is determined by the firm's competitive strategy. If a firm is competing on customized services, customers must be allowed at least the perception that they can control some components of the process.

ENHANCING YOUR CUSTOMERS' PERCEIVED CONTROL

The service provider's strategy may allocate control, and customers may not be able to make educated choices, but the struggle to save face and maintain autonomy continues. However, if perception is indeed reality, as an effective political consultant is supposed to have quipped, then cognitive control is often sufficient to disarm the prickly consumer and terminate the battle for control. Each of the following techniques allays doubts and obtains customer cooperation by conveying outcome or process information and thus implying that the customer has control.

1. Frame the Encounter

Framing—depicting or presenting—the options cleverly can help service providers achieve the desired outcome by motivating the consumer to take a particular action. Healthcare professionals regularly frame patient decisions in a way that achieves the result they want. The cleverness comes in when the provider selects the most effective information to include and assesses the recipient's susceptibility to *gain-framed* (positive) or *loss-framed* (negative) messages. When the consequences of a patient's habits are potentially life-threatening, research shows that treatment results presented in a negative light are more likely to be followed. This means people are more likely to quit smoking if they are told that if they don't stop, they will die in five years, as opposed to saying that they will live five years more if they do stop. In less extreme situations, the effectiveness of the frame depends upon the outlook of the customers—whether they are gain- or loss-oriented. For example, one study found that patients in a dental care service who were gain-oriented responded favorably to the positively framed message promoting preventive care: "Flossing will lead to healthy gums and teeth." Patients who were loss-oriented responded better when the dentist said, "Not flossing will lead to gum disease and decay and will result in teeth extraction."[7]

In typical business situations, managers are well advised to frame an issue in terms that describe the glass as half full rather than half empty. Staff members are more likely to feel motivated to increase their efforts when they hear, "Thirty of the last fifty products have made a profit," as opposed to, "Twenty of the last fifty products have lost money." The positive emphasis is essential to stimulating an entrepreneurial, energetic attitude among the members of the workforce.

2. Structure the Choice

As we mentioned, people can be overwhelmed by choice in a society marked by wide selections of everything from cereals to insurance plans. *The Paradox of Choice*, a recent book by Barry Schwartz, develops the argument that less is more. He explains how humans react: "as the number of options under consideration goes up and the attractive features associated with the rejected alternatives accumulate, the satisfaction derived from the chosen alternative will go down."[8] More options take more time to evaluate. We begin to experience feelings of regret or downright loss. We start thinking that we made the wrong choice. In fact, even when an option is reversible—we can return the sofa or change our vacation plans within 30 days—we still stew over the choices and fail to fully enjoy the selections made.

For service managers, the issue is to put themselves in the place of the overwhelmed customer who is making decisions. Ideally, the choice problem can be mitigated by adopting processes that make the customer comfortable, align with the customer's expectation of options, and move the encounter efficiently. Choice overload frustration can be particularly upsetting to elderly people who have been coping with mounting change (gain and loss), information, technologies, and interactions with new people for decades. The savvy manager will learn the preferences and goals of older customers and have the service reps present a limited number of appropriate choices, whether they are buying laptops or Medicare Advantage plans.

A Menu of Infinite Choices

A customer comes into a restaurant drawn by an advertisement promising "a truly unlimited menu for the discriminating diner." After considering the possibilities for some time, the diner is ready to place his order:

> Waiter: Sir, what would you like from our fabulous kitchen this evening? Can I order you a starter?
>
> Diner: I'd like the French onion soup.
>
> Waiter: A fine choice, indeed. However, the turtle soup is exceptional today.
>
> Diner: Okay. Sure.
>
> Waiter: And what would you like for your main course?
>
> Diner: A New York steak, rare, please.
>
> Waiter: The New York steak is always excellent, but the chef has a spectacular top sirloin tonight. It's not to be missed. It is best served medium rare.
>
> Diner: Well, that does sound good. I'll go with that then—medium rare.
>
> Waiter: And for desert?
>
> Diner: Banana cream pie, please.
>
> Waiter: Of course. Oh, have you ever tried our tiramisu? It really is not to be missed!
>
> Diner: Gosh, if it's not to be missed, then I'll go with that too.

The waiter walks into the kitchen and calls out to the chef, "One number 3!"

3. Choose the Default Carefully

When you download an update for Skype, an Internet-based communication tool, you are asked to make a number of decisions, such as selecting the default browser or search engine. In other instances when you register for a web service such as TicketMaster to buy concert tickets, you are asked if you want to receive e-mails about upcoming events. Although customers have a choice for opting in or out of the weekly e-mails, a vast majority go with the default. The problem of sticking with the default is not restricted to trivial decisions like receiving e-mails but extends to extremely important decisions like participation in retirement plans. A vast majority of employees do not participate in retirement plans when they are asked to enroll in one. In other words if the default decision is not to participate, then participation rates are low. A simple but effective strategy is automatically enrolling employees in the retirement plan.[9] Consequently, instead of needing to actively enroll, employees would need to actively opt out of the company retirement plan, which they seldom do.

4. Preview the Service Realistically

Realistic service previews emotionally prepare the customer for the service and facilitate its delivery. The preview engenders a déjà vu–like feeling of having obtained the service before, thus enhancing cognitive control. Cosmetic surgeons give their customers DVDs explaining types of elective procedures and surgical techniques and describing the outcomes they can expect. Bumrungrad International Hospital, a leading multispecialty medical center in Bangkok serving patients from all over the world, connects prospective patients with recent patients who have similar backgrounds. This allows people to get firsthand information specific to their concerns. Cruise lines post online videos highlighting services available during the cruise. The videos enhance the explicit feeling of control because guests can make plans in advance. They also dispense with the once requisite orientation lecture in the main lounge, which frees up passengers to get on with having fun.

5. Offer Outcome Information

Making information available to customers is central to managing cognitive control. Service providers have a good idea of what customers want from the encounter and can supply information about the impending outcome.

> "After I update your account, wait about four hours and then your television will begin offering your new channels."

> "When we finish here, the charge will be gone from your card."

> "You are saving $110 on your limited series performance, and I am including a voucher for a complimentary glass of wine before each show."

Although it might seem helpful for service providers to give customers as much information as they have available, there are situations in which more information is not necessarily better, and may even be worse. Outcomes that generate strongly positive or negative emotions must be handled with care. For example, some terminally ill patients don't want details about their prognosis. Likewise, in the wake of a stock market decline, many investors prefer not to be reminded of the shrinking value of their retirement savings. In such situations, it's often possible to let people choose how much information they will receive. Web technologies are well-suited to customized data delivery, allowing individuals to access as much or as little information as they want.

6. Provide Information About Progress

Letting people know where they stand in the system gives them at least some sense of control. At Disneyland, signs tell people waiting in line for the rides how long they can expect to wait "from this point." FedEx real-time package tracking conveys travel progress online from warehouse to truck. Customer frustration intensifies, however, when the information is too limited to be useful, as when the telephone company promises to make a repair call within an eight-hour period during the day and never updates the information as time passes. After a few hours, customers begin to wonder if they've been forgotten.

DEVISE MISTAKE-PROOF PROCESSES

No presentation of control is complete without a discussion of *poka-yokes*, which are special procedures and tools that can be used to prevent errors and that can control customer and server actions. In the 1960s, Japanese industrial engineer Shigeo Shingo designed simple tools and techniques to help Toyota achieve zero defects in the company's manufacturing processes. He called the concept and the mechanisms "poka-yoke," or "mistake-proofing." To visualize the concept, consider the many cords that plug into a desktop computer where each type fits only into the appropriate receptacle. At Toyota, virtually every aspect of vehicle construction uses multiple poka-yoke devices to ensure against operator error, including fixtures that align parts, light beams that stop the machine if a worker sticks a hand in the way, clamps that turn in only one direction, and parts kits for the components used in a particular assembly.

In services, poka-yoke mechanisms are surprisingly common and may control customer as well as server actions. Many of them are familiar:

- Metal frames measuring carry-on luggage at the airport check-in

- Signs showing that the airline lavatory is occupied when the door locks

- Hand-carried buzzers letting people at restaurants know when their table is ready

- Baristas writing the customer's name on the coffee cup and checking off the coffee order at Starbucks

- Indented hospital instrument trays ensuring that no instruments are left in the patient after surgery

- Automatic call systems alerting staff members at the nursing station when a patient's heart rate has gone above or below specified limits

Employees come up with many poka-yokes themselves. Childcare center staff members came up with the idea of drawing toy outlines on the walls and floors to show the children where to put the toys when they've finished playing with them. One childcare consultant even advocates posting photographs by the door to show what a "clean" room really looks like. Managers at Seoul Land amusement park in Seoul, South Korea, thought that sewing shut the pants pockets on male worker uniforms would effectively prevent the men from slouching on the job. (We are just reporting here.)

Finally, a major hotel chain applies a novel poka-yoke fail-safe to acknowledge repeat customers. When the bellhop greets arriving guests and carries their luggage inside, he asks whether this is their first stay. If the guests reply that they've been there before, the bellhop discreetly tugs his ear in sight of the front desk clerk, who then greets the guests with a hearty "Welcome back!"

MANAGE SERVER BEHAVIOR

Poka-yoke thinking is reflected in behavioral management techniques for controlling server behavior. In fact, the essence of behavioral management is establishing explicit cues and consequences for desired actions. Even such soft concepts as friendliness can be rendered mistake-proof to some degree with:

- Mirrors next to call center phones prompting a "smiling" voice from the reps

- Banks ensuring eye contact by having tellers record customer eye color

The operant term is *explicit*, since general admonitions such as "be friendly" aren't very useful guides to action. Fast-food chains emphasize the importance of customer service but don't always identify specific, on-the-job cues or payoffs to encourage friendliness toward customers.[10] A research team exploring the issue designated four moments in the service encounter as cues to smile, the basic signal of friendliness: when greeting the customer, taking the order, telling the customer about the dessert special, and giving the customer change. It encouraged the employees to observe the consequence of their smiles, specifically whether customers smiled back, thus reinforcing the friendliness of the encounter. Supervisors provided a second consequence in the form of praise and recognition. The researchers asked the supervisors to recognize each employee's smiling behavior at least once a day and to keep a record documenting their own recognition behavior. A second basic signal of friendliness, talking with the customer, was also built into the transactions. Employees memorized opening lines ranging from information about the menu to inquiries about customer preferences. They also learned to recognize social cues for initiating talk, and supervisors provided daily recognition of good performance.

SWAY WITH SOCIAL PROOFING

Another technique for eliciting the desired customer response is the pressure to conform called *social proofing*. Social proofing describes a phenomenon in which people who are unsure about the appropriate action copy that of other participants in the same situation. Service providers can often apply the phenomenon effectively by showing customers that other people have complied with a request. A common example is the discovery that hotel guests are likelier to reuse their towels when the sign in the hotel bathroom says, "Join your fellow guests in helping to save the environment. Almost 75 percent of [our hotel] guests use their towels more than once," than when the sign says, "Keep our environment green."

The effect was even stronger when guests were told that *75 percent of those who had previously stayed in their room* had reused a towel.[11]

CONCLUSION

We believe that service quality efforts and CRM have missed the boat when it comes to understanding ways to achieve control and enhance customer perceptions of feeling in control. As with other areas of customer experiences we've outlined in this book, rectifying the problem first requires an understanding of the psychology behind the concepts. Second, it requires an appreciation for enhancing customer perceptions of control and thus enhancing customer satisfaction. Considerable evidence attesting to the value of giving the customer the perception of control has been compiled in healthcare studies, but there has not been nearly as much data compiled to date in the business world. Most companies more or less seem to stumble across perceived control by accident and recognize its benefits in a hit-or-miss fashion. Third, correcting the problem requires managers to carefully analyze their service operations to find out where the concepts can be applied. To this end, we propose that service providers develop a *customer control audit*, which entails examining each step in the service delivery process using the emotion prints discussed in Chapter 2, "Designing Emotionally Intelligent Processes," and identifying where it makes sense to enhance the customer's perception of control. Tapping customer perspectives informed by the trade-offs described in determining the locus of control can help providers refine their awareness of the extent to which this is possible, and framing could be used to make specific modifications. The following five principles can be employed to guide these modifications.

Principles of Control and Choice

1. **Frame messages about options according to a customer's outlook on life.** Gain-oriented people are more likely to respond to positively framed messages, while loss-oriented people are more likely to respond to negatively-framed messages. Of course, finding which category people fall into is often the challenge.

2. **Create an illusion of control.** Even if you can't provide actual, hands-on control for a customer, there are usually places in a service encounter, such as maintaining an orderly waiting line process, that can make the customer feel that events are under rational control *by somebody*.

3. **Look for places to cede control.** Enterprise Rent-A-Car advertises that its preferred customers can walk down the row of cars and pick the car they want; many cruise lines allow total flexibility in deciding when and where passengers take their meals.

4. **Limit choices.** An apocryphal finding from a lab study of rats is that when confronted with too many choices, behavior becomes random. While humans rarely become so flummoxed, we often feel overwhelmed when making decisions about such things as medical plans. This is particularly true for seniors.

5. **Control your customers.** In many services, customers are the source of the problem. In a study of critical incidents from hotel, airlines, and restaurants, Bitner and her coauthors[12] found that 22 percent of the bad experiences were the result of bad behavior by customers.

SEQUENCING THE EXPERIENCE

If you don't have a strong finish to a film, you are in serious trouble. It can be explosive. It can be a bang or a whimper, but it better be memorable, or else people will remember very little about the movie. If a movie has a riveting conclusion, audiences are happy to overlook earlier flaws. By contrast, if the picture has a bummer of an ending, people forget almost everything they liked about the film.

—Robert Towne, Screenwriter[1]

Imagine that the organizers of a Fourth of July pyrotechnics display, in a moment of exuberance, decided to reverse the order in which they trigger the fireworks. They would present exactly the same show but as if it were in rewind. It simply wouldn't be the same experience. The climax would come first with its dozens of simultaneous bursts, and the show would finish with individual rockets and mortars. On the basis of sequence, two service encounters that are identical in terms of process outcomes, information conveyed, and courtesy extended by the server can generate similarly different levels of excitement in the eyes of the customer.

From the perspective of the service providers, the difference may seem like a paradox. But behavioral scientists have found the answer by examining the way people summarize events that contribute to a whole experience.[2] For service design, the implications of their findings are clear: we want to organize the sequence of events so that the encounter is perceived positively while it is taking place, and we want to make sure that it's recalled positively after it's completed.

THE SEQUENCE IMPACTS YOUR CUSTOMERS' PERCEPTIONS

A theme park visit consists of a multitude of events that encompass waiting, going on rides, resting, walking, eating, and buying. Wow, that was a long day. Rehashing the visit during the drive home, you might wonder, "Was every minute equally fun?" Everyone's exhausted. The day's a blur. The roller coaster was far better than the one you rode at the state fair when you were a kid. After a week or so, you probably recall a few moments vividly, and the rest is more difficult to reconstruct or is simply forgotten. You remember the kid dumping his sno-cone on your shoe, and you smile about the roller coaster. Chances are you didn't keep track of every trip to the restroom or water fountain, every line you stood in, and every snack you bought. You might not even remember every ride you rode. This is because memories aren't movies; they're more like a collection of snapshots.

Peak and End Rule

Thinking back on the theme park, you may sort these snapshots into a mental photo album of the experience. If someone asks you how it went, you might express a liking or disliking for the experience, but it's entirely possible that you don't know exactly why you feel the way you do. For a long time, behaviorists have assumed that we simply keep score by associating feelings with each event, weighting every event equally, and then adding them up. It turns out—probably to no one's surprise if you think about it—that all moments are not equally important.

One factor that influences our assessment is the meaning we give to the experience, such as, "It was great because I was able to spend time with my son." Pressed for details, we may respond by describing individual aspects that stood out, not all of which may be objectively considered important. Our memory may consist of some very mundane events or images—the waiter at the restaurant had strange eyebrows, the marigolds were brilliant, there was chewing gum on the table—along with some highs and lows. The high point may be the adrenaline rush you felt on the roller coaster, and the low point may be a truly boring experience in some boat floating through a stupid tunnel or that sticky sno-cone leaking into your shoe. The influence of each event on our overall assessment is difficult for us to discern. We may not store the details of the peak and the low point but merely how we felt during those highs and lows. In other words, the summary assessment of the experience is based on a handful of emotional moments and snapshots that are somehow combined or pooled.

Our assessment is an amalgamation of the ending, highs and lows, beginning, and trends that developed throughout the experience. How we combine these factors, in particular the role of the ending, goes against logic, at least on the surface. For example, believe it or not, we may prefer more pain provided that the ending is better. This is known as the *peak and end rule*. You may have heard about this famous study:

> Subjects were exposed to two aversive experiences: in the short trial, they immersed one hand in water at 14°C [57.5°F] for 60 s; in the long trial, they immersed the other hand at 14°C for 60 s, then kept the hand in the water 30 s longer as the temperature of the water was gradually raised to 15°C, still painful but distinctly less so for most subjects. Subjects were later given a choice of which trial to repeat. A significant majority chose to repeat the long trial, apparently preferring more pain over less.[3]

Although the choice seems surprising at first, entertainers have known for a long time the importance of a big finish. Rock concerts always conclude with hits, comedians save their best jokes for the end, and the Fourth of July fireworks display closes with a deafening finale. Redelmeier and Kahneman conducted a field experiment to validate their laboratory findings (see Colonoscopy Study).

Colonoscopy Study

Looking at the two graphs in the figure, who do you think—patient A or B—would recall the experience as being less painful? Strange as it might seem, patient B remembers it as less painful than A does, even though B underwent the procedure for twice as long. The reason lies in the peak and end rule, which holds that total remembered discomfort is largely determined by the intensity of discomfort at the worst part and at the final part of the event. Although the peak level of pain was the same for both patients, the ending for patient B could be characterized as a soft landing, whereas for patient A, the peak level of pain occurred right at the end of the whole ordeal. We can roughly measure emotional satisfaction with an encounter by taking the average of emotions at the peak and at or near the end of the encounter.

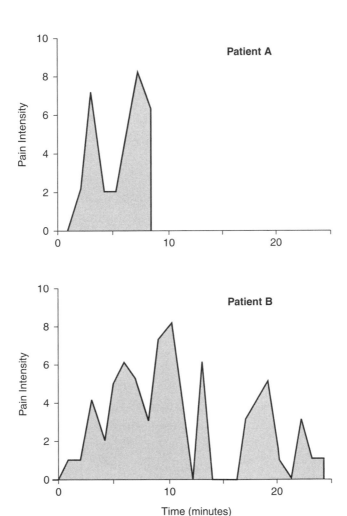

Real-time recordings from two patients. Each group displays the intensity of pain recorded each minute by a patient undergoing colonoscopy. The experiences of two individuals are shown (Patient A and Patient B). The x-axis represents time in minutes from the start of the procedure. The y-axis represents the intensity of pain recorded in real-time on a visual analogue scale with ends denoted as "no pain" and "extreme pain." The procedure lasted 8 min for Patient A and 24 min for Patient B.

Highs and Lows

In addition to the ending, the high points and the low points of an experience also have a disproportionately large impact on our overall assessment. The impact of the highs and lows is more obvious than that of the ending. That roller coaster ride was especially intense, and within it, there was the hesitation at the top before the breathtaking plunge almost straight down. A negative incident can just as effectively sear itself into the brain. How many times have you heard someone rant, "The whole evening was ruined by . . ."? One low moment can wreck an experience and dominate the memory of it for a long time.

The Beginning

Everyone has heard the old saw, "You only get one chance to make a first impression." We have argued that the last event is very important, but, clearly, so is the first. As to the relative significance of the start, one of the major contentions in traditional service encounter design is that the beginning and the end of a service encounter—the so-called service bookends—are equally important.

A bad start can determine how you process the rest of the experience. Imagine you get off a long flight, grab a taxi, and finally get to your hotel at 11 p.m. The desk clerk ignores you and keeps talking on his cell for a couple of minutes before reluctantly checking you in. Luckily the hotel dining room is still open, so you drop your bags in your room and dash down to grab a bite. The food is fine, but the server makes an error on the bill, and you have to hang around to get it resolved. Would your feelings about the error be the same if the front desk experience had been positive? Probably not.

As to whether the start and finish of an encounter are equal, it depends. In general, we contend that the strategy of finishing stronger than you start is a sound one. Let's keep going with that hotel arrival. Suppose the rest of your stay goes well, you get a complimentary room service breakfast, and the checkout clerk is exceptionally polite. Imagine a second scenario in which check-in goes smoothly, the clerk is exceptionally pleasant and welcoming, and the rest of the stay is similar to that in the first scenario. This time, however, you have problems checking out. The clerk is indifferent and keeps you and two others waiting. It takes you a long time to check out. Are the feelings about the two scenarios the same? Again, probably not.

Again, according to the peak and end rule, the negative event at the end darkens the second scenario for a considerably more negative overall assessment than the beginning did in the first scenario. Even if we were to discount the ice water study's claim that the ending influences our final assessment more than the beginning does, other practical considerations influence the relative significance of the front end and the finish. A bad start gives the service provider time to make things right. In the first scenario, you may have complained to the manager, who apologized and provided the complimentary room service breakfast as token compensation for your distress. In the second scenario, if nothing else, the hotel has less time to mount a recovery.

The beginning has the greatest impact on first-time customers, especially if they can easily switch to a competitor. If you go to a drop-in hair salon and the receptionist ignores you by talking on the phone while you stand there, you may turn around and walk out. The front end will also be important for repeat customers who will be skeptical if their prior experiences have been poor or the baseline trust in the firm or in the industry is low. The front end is especially important when the customer is anxious or needs immediate attention. Emergency rooms have long struggled with greeting everyone respectfully while prioritizing the truly emergent cases. The front end also plays a major role in complex services like education, where customers have to be informed about the rules and procedures. At USC's Marshall School of Business, as in other leading schools, great effort goes into orientation pro-grams for incoming MBA students.

Trends and the Extrapolation Effect

Our perceptions of an experience are strongly influenced by trends that we may never articulate. We definitely prefer upward trends. Think about a movie that starts slowly and picks up as compared to one that starts out strong and then fades out. The idea of run-ning the Fourth of July fireworks display backwards makes the same point. Not surprisingly, we like encounters that improve rap-idly even more. We especially like trends that improve rapidly near the end.

Trends are important because we use them to predict future performance. Basing forecasts on short-term trends is sometimes referred to as the *extrapolation effect*. A patient who has been going through a long and painful medical experience, for example, may respond to a trend of decreasing pain by extrapolating a future that is less painful and even inferring that he or she is getting close to a full recovery. The trend that gets better may also improve the transient experience itself by reducing dread or increasing positive anticipa-tion. The patient on the slow road to recovery, for example, is put in a more positive mindset simply by imagining that the experience is going to get better.

Sports fans take the extrapolation effect to absurd lengths dur-ing playoffs. If the Lakers lose the first game in a series by 20 points, many fans rashly abandon all hope and become unable to see how their team can possibly win the next game, let alone the series. If the team wins the next game, however, these same fans suddenly can't imagine the Lakers losing another game, let alone the series. An implication that flows from the extrapolation effect for service pro-viders is that an improving trend, particularly toward the end, may cause the customer to expect an even better experience the next time around. This belief can increase the chance of a revisit or at least sellouts for the next game.

CUSTOMERS' PREFERENCES FOR SEPARATING OR COMBINING EVENTS

Another set of factors that bears on service encounter design deals with our preferences for separating or combining emotionally powerful events. A number of factors can affect the impact of the sequence and thus the preference:

- Two negative events (e.g., losing bids on two contracts) on the same day or on different days

- Two positive events (e.g., winning two bids) on the same or on different days

- A mixture of positive and negative events each day

- Good news in the morning and bad news in the afternoon, or vice versa

We predicate our preferences on the importance we place on the gains and losses and on our cognitive capacity to savor gains and cope with losses. When it comes to savoring gains, it would seem that piling positive events on top of one another should not be a concern. The reality, however, is that we don't enjoy each one as fully as we would if they came separately. For one thing, positive events occurring close together in time frequently act as substitutes for one another. Furthermore, your parents were right; it is possible to have too much of a good thing. Celebrating the first event may diminish the impact of the second and possibly the pleasure of the first one as well. We also usually would rather break up positive events, preferring, for example, to receive two $10 gift certificates rather than one $20 gift certificate.

With respect to coping with losses, if the losses are small, we prefer to combine them. Hit me with the bad news all at once! On the other hand, if the impact of two losses is big, then we prefer that they be separated. The primary reason for putting some time between large losses is that people are trying to replenish their reserves of emotional strength after the first loss with the expectation that they then will be able to manage the second one better.

As to mixing gains and losses—given that losses are expected—we like to pair small gains with large losses. Even tiny gains help buffer the distress caused by the big loss. Harrah's casino has learned by mining data about its customers' habits that when gamblers are having a losing streak, small "comps" encourage them to keep gambling despite their losses. A healthier example comes from Weight Watchers testimony. People eventually hit a dreaded weight-loss plateau, during which the pounds quit disappearing despite the dieters sticking closely to the meal plan. Rather than give up or become even more restrictive, a number of dieters find that allowing themselves a controlled temporary indulgence puts the program back on track. It's as if their bodies wanted a little reward to keep burning off the calories! People also prefer to combine a small loss with a large gain, since good news overshadows the bad on any given day, whereas if separated, the small loss would stand out more strongly in retrospect.

When it comes to the order of things, if we are to receive good news and bad news, we inevitably want the bad news first. We dread bad news, and we want to know right away, whereas we may enjoy the anticipating good news. Hence waiting for good news can be fun.

SEQUENCING WHEN THERE ARE MULTIPLE ENCOUNTERS

So far we've talked as if an entire experience always occurs in a continuous block of time. This may be true for a movie, rock concert, dentist visit, vacation, or stay at a hotel. There are many services, however, that involve repeat visits with a service provider. They involve sequence effects if one encounter depends on the next.

Repeat visits fall into two broad categories. One is exemplified by supermarkets. We visit the supermarket many times, but our visits aren't strongly connected, so we'll call these *independent encounters*.

College courses exemplify another type of service experience with multiple visits. For a single course during the semester, students attend many classes. These classes are linked because they are all directed toward a common goal tied to the subject matter, so we call them *dependent encounters*. Other examples of dependent encounters include curative radiation therapy, physical therapy following hip replacement surgery, pregnancy, home buying, and divorce proceedings. All have a single goal.

Sequence effects—peak and end, highs and lows, beginning and end—affect our assessments of dependent encounters. A study of obstetrics patients found that a handful of events dominated the recollection of care during pregnancy.[4] The dominating events were all highs and lows. One high point during the pregnancy was the ultrasound imaging of the baby. Another, of course, was the birth of the baby. Some of the mothers in our study reported negative experiences, such as a rude nurse during the delivery. Even when these events occurred many years earlier, the bad memory continued to be vivid and emotionally charged as if it were yesterday, illustrating the power of the peak event on long-term recall.

For services comprising independent encounters, the perception of a positive trend may cause us to return for a repeat experience. Once we've gone through the experience a few times, though, the sequence effect based on trends or even resulting from variations (highs and lows) among encounters evaporates. After each one, customers may reevaluate the service provider, but that's likely to occur only if something happened to distinguish one experience from another. Even so, customers who have repeatedly used a service provider don't react as strongly as new customers do to one or two aberrations in service. Even in as problematic a service domain as cellular telephones, customers who had a long history with a particular wireless service provider lagged behind new customers when it came to updating their customer service ratings following a bad experience.[5] Managers can parlay this finding into using the longer window they have with established customers to redeem themselves and focus on acting quickly to secure the loyalty of a new customer who might be ready to jump ship after a negative encounter.

DESIGNING THE SEQUENCE

Sequence characteristics are critical to designing service encounters that exploit our tendency to recollect events as snapshots and maximize positive emotional elements. Having examined the importance of designing service encounters that take emotions, trust, and control into account, we are ready to incorporate everything into sequences of events that take place during the encounter process.

Build a Positive Trend and End on a High Note

It's easiest (but not necessarily easy) to control the trends and endings if you are an entertainment director. Movie scripts, rock concerts, comedy shows, and cruise line vacations can be designed to demonstrate positive trends and to end on high notes. One filmmaker freely shared his approach to designing the flow of a film. He grabs the audience right away and sets the goal for the protagonist. The audience is on board with the mission by the end of the first half-hour—whether it's saving the orphans, finding the treasure, or thawing the bitter but tender-hearted millionaire. Then he lets the storyline cruise to about the two-thirds point at which time, suddenly, all is lost. He then jacks up the action (creates an improving trend) and, with the tempo of the soundtrack and audience excitement increasing, salvages the mission at the climax (peak) and brings it to a swift end, which he describes as being like a "Fourth of July fireworks show." The director does this in film after film, because he says, "That's the pattern that we as moviegoers like, and that's the pattern we want." So that's the pattern we get.

Cruise lines like to end each day on a high note with raffles, shows, and contests, as if the day was a uniquely exhilarating holiday for everyone involved (even if it's just another workday for the crew). Packing a multitude of discrete festivities into a fairly short vacation engenders the feeling that the vacation is longer than it actually is.

They even sequence the ports of call so as to create the sense of a trend and get the most out of watching a glacier calve or swimming with dolphins or hiking through Roman ruins. On the final night of the cruise, the traditional captain's dinner is designed to crank the excitement and the impression of exclusive luxury up several notches and end on a truly glass-breaking high note.

Back on the ground, so to speak, a corporate travel agent described her planning process with corporate clients. She always greets the clients enthusiastically, inquires politely about their most recent trips, and then asks what they want from their forthcoming trips. Her pattern is to suggest a good flight time and good hotel, and then, after brief reflection, to propose a better flight time and a better hotel, often at the same price or less. She proceeds to describe something memorable about the accommodations, like the room is on the twenty-third floor, facing Central Park. She also mentions some special event that might be going on that day in that city, such as a colorful ethnic festival. She closes with value-added benefits, perhaps an upgrade from business class to first class or a couple of free tickets to the car show that day. The payoff is reliable repeat business from a Rolodex full of satisfied corporate executives.

Even call center conversations and face-to-face retail interactions with first-time customers can be carefully constructed to leverage the sequence effects. A First Republic Bank branch manager described the sequence his organization applies from beginning to end to foster an emotional theme built on relationship banking. When a new customer enters the bank, a teller greets her with a warm and friendly handshake and escorts her to a desk. First Republic branches create an especially comfortable atmosphere by having small staffs of three to five people sit at desks instead of standing at teller windows. When all tellers are busy, a staff member still acknowledges the customer and invites her to take a comfortable seat near a table set with a tray of freshly baked cookies. When a new customer's business nears completion, the teller introduces him or her to the other staff members. All staff members at that branch are informed about the customer's needs and background so that, in the future, any staff member can provide help. At the end of that first visit, the teller shakes the customer's hand again and thanks him or her for the business. The relationship focus is carried forward to subsequent visits, during which the customer is always greeted by name.

It is now common practice for the better trade shows to get unpleasant tasks out of the way before the service begins. They encourage online attendee preregistration that integrates as many of the boring paperwork steps as possible. When attendees arrive, they simply pick up a badge that has been programmed with their personal data. The badge allows them to exchange information at any booth, just by swiping it through an electronic reader, thus avoiding an endless exchange of business cards and sign-in sheets. The events that attendees enjoy and come to see, such as product demos, are plentiful, and they're located along pathways that draw visitors through the venue.

Many consulting firms already know (perhaps intuitively) how to construct a *multiperiod sequence flow*. Typically, the first encounters begin with measured enthusiasm sprinkled with a few obvious (to them at least) nuggets that help close the deal. This is followed by multiple encounters entailing observations, interviews, and back-office analyses. These constitute the cruising phase of a project, the time that makes up the encounter that is not part of the peak. They then pick up the pace with increasingly good proposals and finish with a bang by providing the most valuable gold nuggets right at the end. Sounds like a pretty good movie.

There are nuances to the multiperiod sequence flow strategy of course. A statistician friend of ours accidentally discovered the benefit of waiting until the end to offer the golden nugget. He had been hired to tease out the factors that explained the success of a new video game. His clients agreed at the start that the project would accomplish their goals if the consultant's model could explain just 6 percent of the variability in sales among a dozen competing video games. The statistician made progress over the first three months of

SEQUENCING THE EXPERIENCE 131

the project, but he didn't report on it until he was finished. To his profound satisfaction—and he didn't delay his results intentionally—on the very last day, his analysis yielded a three-factor combination that explained more than *90 percent* of the variability in sales: beta testing with gamers, advertising, and number of sales outlets. Because it came at the end, this positive surprise had far more impact than it would have had at the outset because the clients' longer-term involvement had sensitized them to the complexity of the task.

Combine Losses and Segment Gains

Retailers love to *upsell*, encourage customers to purchase additional upgrades, add-ons, and more expensive items or services. Just try to purchase the rock-bottom, basic package of ballroom dance lessons. When you open a new bank account, brace yourself for employees heavily incentivized to *cross-sell* additional products, such as savings accounts, IRAs, insurance, credit cards, safe deposit boxes, and much more.

When a customer goes in for an oil change, the dilemma for the company providing the service is whether it should combine all its upselling offers or break them up into multiple offers. Our friend Chris tells a story about his encounter with mechanics.

Right to the Bitter End

Chris took his Audi in for an oil change at a Jiffy Lube near Seattle. Several "mechanics" were minding the store. A few minutes after he drove his car into the bay, one of the mechanics walked up to Chris and asked him if he would like to upgrade the quality of the engine oil. The mechanic said he recommended this $20 upgrade because it was designed for an Audi. Chris agreed to the upgrade. Two minutes later, another mechanic showed him his dirty air filter and offered to replace it for an additional charge of $20.

Chris declined that one. Three minutes later, yet a third mechanic pointed out some tiny dings in the windshield and said that he could repair them for $5, which would cover the copayment to his insurance company that would cover the balance of the actual cost. Chris didn't have his insurance information with him, so the possibility of having his insurance pay fell through. A couple of minutes later, a fourth mechanic came up to Chris and quoted $60 to fix the windshield. By this time Chris was exasperated, and he muttered out loud, "They don't stop going after your wallet, do they?" His comment inspired all the other customers in the store to join in and create a chorus of complaints.

Raise the Lows and the Highs

In order to exploit the sequence effect, we often need to reorganize the events to push the highs to their maximum and minimize the lows. In some cases this is possible (Hollywood movies), in some it isn't (dental procedures), and sometimes it's just complicated. That's when you take a look at the peaks and valleys and do what you can to adjust them. Chris Ullman, a chiropractor in Manhattan Beach, California, provides massage as part of his treatment routine. Clients generally prefer to receive the massage at the end of the session, since they go home in a state of peak relaxation. The massage therapist and the chiropractor prefer to give the massage at the start, because it loosens up the muscles and facilitates the adjustment. If the clinic lets clients choose to receive the massage last, the solution may be to tweak the highs (relaxation) and lows (painful adjustment), perhaps by putting waiting clients into a vibrating chair or giving them an ice pack or a heating pad, whichever relaxes their muscles.

Processes that cannot be re-sequenced can at least be submitted to an examination of the highs and lows embedded in them. Standard process improvement methods focus solely on the lows, but sequence theory says you can profit from improving the highs as well.

SEQUENCE THEORY MATTERS FOR YOUR EMPLOYEES

In addition to the service encounter, sequence theory applies to many other human interactions in business, such as performance appraisals, staff meetings, and training programs. Outside of business, sequence theory applies to such interactions as psychological counseling and lesson planning for teachers.

When performing employee performance reviews, for example, evaluators may be able to help struggling employees respond more productively by spreading out strongly critical feedback over multiple short meetings rather than dumping it on them all at once. Segmenting significant pain actually helps to lessen it. During the individual sessions, moreover, evaluators should also offer some positive feedback as an emotional buffer that establishes a positive trend. Similarly, when evaluators have several pieces of great feedback, it might make sense to spread these out over a couple of shorter meetings rather than use them up all at once.

In staff meetings, it is typical for the boss to start off with a brief comment about how the group is doing a good job. This is followed by a litany of failures, albeit sweetened with a sprinkling of positive comments, and an ending that exhorts the team to greater effort and accomplishments. A more productive way to manage the meeting is to heavily highlight positive results near the end, thereby providing a better launch pad for firing up the team to greater heights.

Training programs make an effort to distinguish sequence flows within, say, a one-day period and also throughout extended programs covering multiple days. For both types of courses, the ideas presented about positive trends readily apply. The one-day session would end the morning portion on a high note as a way to stimulate excitement for the upcoming afternoon session. The rest of the day would build to a close that included attendees demonstrating their learning and the closing would reinforce the good effort that they have shown. Although it is difficult to generalize across all kinds of programs, professional trainers invariably find that mixing the types of activities—lecture, demo, hands-on, role play—is fundamental to the structure of a successful day. For extended programs, it is important to emphasize the building blocks in place at the end of each day and to reinforce the progress made toward a clear objective, like certification. The last event of the final day should include a celebration and good-natured awards for the participants.

Noted West Coast clinical psychologist Jane Wick in an interview described her practice process to illustrate sequence concepts that can be employed in patient programs. At the start, she assesses the patients' emotions and uses her assessment to guide each of her responses. If they appear to be fairly relaxed, she asks, "How's it going today?" Then she helps patients explore issues as they arise. If patients are clearly distraught, she asks them to discuss what's bothering them. As they do, she responds empathetically, mirroring the patients' feelings: "Oh, oh, how awful." As the 50-minute session nears its end, she winds it down, soothing the patients' emotions, so that, "They feel put together, not undone." At the closing, she makes a point of letting them know that she is very interested by recalling something they said earlier in the conversation in order to indicate that she really heard them.

PRINCIPLES FOR SEQUENCING THE ENCOUNTER

Managers need to view every aspect of their organization's interactions with customers and employees as sequences that can be managed. In general terms, you want to map the flow, look for peaks and valleys, and be cognizant of the relative importance of the beginning and the end. The way to think about sequences is as pieces of a story that will be scripted in such a way as to generate positive memories for the customer. In arranging these pieces, we propose five principles:

1. **Finish strong.** Ending on a high note is an important aspect of almost every service encounter. The mantra of gymnastics, "Stick the dismount," should be the mantra of businesses as well.

2. **Build an improving trend.** People like things to keep moving in a positive direction. Thus, all things being equal, it is better to start a little lower and build a little higher than to start a little higher and fall off a little at the end. Of course, a faster positive trend takes advantage of the "extrapolation effect."

3. **Create a peak.** If you want to improve the perception of your service, you are better off making one step sensational and the other steps merely adequate. Sea World could spend a lot more money on attractions, but the thing that counts—the signature Shamu the Whale show—must be done to perfection.

4. **Get bad experiences over with early.** Unpleasant news, discomfort, and unavoidably long waits in line should be the first parts of an experience, not the last. This way, customers avoid the dread of pain or aggravation, and the experiences are less likely to dominate their memory of the entire encounter.

5. **Segment pleasure; combine pain.** Since an event seems longer when it's segmented, service providers should extend the feeling of pleasurable experiences by dividing them and condense unpleasant experiences into a single event.

SELF QUIZ: DSL HELP DESK

Here is a little quiz that we have given to our students.

Which of the following scenarios is likely to generate greater satisfaction?

Scenario 1

    CSR: Hello. How may I help you?

    Caller: I have not been able to connect to the Internet.

    CSR: What is your phone number?

    Caller: I have already given it three times!

    CSR (rather abruptly): Not to me! I can't help you if you don't give me the number. Let's not waste time.

Caller then gives the number. The rest of the conversation is professional and polite. The CSR correctly diagnoses the problem and guides the caller through the corrective steps. Finally, the CSR asks the caller to reboot the computer.

    Caller: If I reboot I will lose some data.

    CSR (very politely): Sir, all you have to do is save the open files and then reboot.

Caller then proceeds to save the files and reboot the computer. The network connection is restored.

    CSR: Thank you for choosing XYZ Inc. I don't expect that you will have any more trouble. If you do have a problem, please call me back at 213-555-1212. This is my direct number. Have a good day.

Scenario 2

    CSR: Hello. How may I help you?

    Caller: I have not been able to connect to the Internet.

    CSR: What is your phone number, sir?

    Caller: I have already given it three times!

    CSR (very politely): I am sorry to hear that, sir. Unfortunately, I don't have access to that information. I need your number to test the network.

Caller then gives the number. The rest of the conversation is professional and polite. The CSR correctly diagnoses the problem and guides the caller through the corrective steps. Finally, the CSR asks the caller to reboot the computer.

> Caller: If I reboot I will lose some data.
> CSR (rather abruptly): All you have to do is save the open files and then reboot. Let's not waste any more time.

Caller then proceeds to save the files and reboot the computer. The network connection is restored.

> CSR (showing clear signs of impatience): I don't expect you will have any more trouble. If you do have a problem, call me back at 213-555-1212. This is my direct number. Goodbye.

Answer: Most prefer the first conversation to the second because of the ending. (Though in both cases, the CSR clearly needs training in customer treatment.)

CHAPTER 6

TIME WARP: DURATION MANAGEMENT

How did it get so late so soon?

—Dr. Seuss

When we have reason to celebrate, we often choose a leisurely dinner at a nice restaurant to mark the occasion. We'll dress more formally than usual, drive some distance, and order elaborate dishes, giving up an entire evening to the meal. As long as the food is good and the companionship is pleasant, the hours don't drag. Attentive servers top off the beverages, supply tasty tidbits, deliver the courses, and pick up on our social cues for more or less interaction, all the while making sure that we know they appreciate our business. Each contact with the wait staff thus adds value to our time at the restaurant as we await the arrival of the main course.

All service encounters, from fine dining to telephone support, encompass sequences of events. Objectively, the experience transpires along an axis of steadily elapsing units of time, but the perception of it is shaped by the rhythm and flow of the events themselves. The role of time and our sense of it depend on whether we, the customers, are waiting for the service encounter or are engaged in it. When we're engaged—that is, interacting with the provider, receiving the service, speaking with a service representative, or witnessing service activity—value-added time is passing. When we're not—that is, when we're waiting—the time is being wasted.

PERCEPTION IS EVERYTHING WHEN IT COMES TO TIME

Looking forward to a vacation, party, sporting event, or family reunion adds to, even extends, the fun. Once, a friend of ours decided to surprise his mother by flying unannounced from his home in Seattle to hers in Bangalore, India. Although his mother was thrilled to see him, she was not happy that he arrived unexpectedly because, by doing so, he deprived her of the pleasure of anticipation. A typical visit from our friend lasts little more than a week, so she relishes those months of looking forward to it. The anticipation itself is part of her engagement in a visit.

That is not the case when we're staring at a wall or screen because we're waiting for a call center agent, a lag in a multiplayer game of World of Warcraft, or a movie downloading from Netflix. In such cases, we chafe at the wasted time and at the sense that it's crawling ever so slowly. Whether or not customers resent or even notice the passage of time during a service encounter, therefore, depends on the nature of their engagement in it. For the customer, perception is everything. Not so for the provider. The actual duration for completing an encounter, however, is a primary determinant of the cost of providing the service.

Upon completing an encounter, the perceived duration strongly affects its value to the customer. Overall, we humans want waits to be short, peaceful moments to be extended, and moments of excitement and anticipation to last just the right amount of time.

Unfortunately, the realities of the service business—capacity, worker skills, nature of the service itself—prohibit organizations from achieving duration nirvana through structural changes. Nevertheless, we can do a better job in each of these areas by making some changes in the process. The key is to understanding how we perceive time and then to use this knowledge to reduce the perceived duration of negative events and increase the perceived duration of positive ones.

TEMPORAL DISTORTIONS

Clearly, our sense of time is subject to considerable distortion. Everyone has been trapped in a tedious situation during which we repeatedly checked the time only to be surprised again and again at how little has elapsed. On the other hand, time seems to fly by when you're working against a deadline. Once the deadline passes, though, you look back at the busy week and find it hard to believe that five whole days have elapsed.

Two basic questions regarding our sense of time are: Do we have an internal clock, and which mental processes help us judge duration? Many biological processes follow a 24-hour daily, or *circadian*, cycle. Our body temperatures, cognitive abilities, and sleep patterns, among other processes, are tuned to the rise and fall of the sun. Carl Linnaeus, the eighteenth-century Swedish botanist who devised our system for naming species, designed a clock using 45 types of flowers that would tell the time via the predictable opening and closing of blossoms throughout the day. Circadian cycles have been found in plants, humans, and other animals even when they are isolated from sunlight. Nonetheless, prolonged cave experiments with human subjects turning the lights on and off for themselves resulted in considerable slip from the solar cycle outside.

Even without the position of the sun being involved, a sense of elapsed time constitutes a significant survival mechanism for many animals. Grazers use a rough sense of time to decide when to move from one grassland to another. William Friedman provides a fascinating description of hummingbirds in Costa Rica perfectly timing their visits to flowers for their nectar. If they return too soon, the flower may not have produced the nectar, and if they wait too long, some other bird may have consumed it.[1] B. F. Skinner's experiments in reinforcement showed that when feeding on a fixed-interval schedule, even laboratory rats have an innate ability to judge duration.[2]

People, too, have an instinct honed by experience for judging the duration of repeated events. One example is the drive to and from the workplace. We know instinctively when the drive takes longer than we think it should. On the other hand, we find it much tougher to gauge the duration of a new experience. For instance, when we're watching a popular Broadway show, we're likely to have no clue how long the second act of *Jersey Boys* lasts. But if one of the singers were to make a tiny error in musical timing, we would find it absolutely jarring because we have a lifelong familiarity with rhythmic structure. Of course, like every other aspect of a service, our feelings affect our perceptions of duration so that our sense of time during the play depends at least partly on whether we hate it and continually check the time, or we like it and pay close attention to what's happening on stage.

The Watched Pot Experiment

In the late 1970s, Richard Block and a couple of colleagues in the psychology department at Montana State University wondered how much the mere act of focusing on the passage of time affects a person's estimation of its duration.[3] They designed an experiment in which each observer spent 270 seconds staring at a beaker of colored liquid sitting on an electrical burner. One group of observers was told that the experiment concerned time perception, and another group heard that it concerned visual perception. The first group was asked to focus on the beaker and, when stopped, to estimate how long they had done so. The second group was asked to observe changes taking place in the liquid and, when stopped, to describe them.

Overall, observers in the time perception group gave longer estimates of duration than those in the visual perception group. The researchers varied the experiment by sometimes interrupting the process with unrelated information and by bringing the liquid to a boil. They found that for those focusing on time, interruptions made the duration seem shorter if the pot did not boil and had no effect if it did. Those recalling visual details, however, sensed that both interruptions and boiling lengthened the duration.

Another layer of complexity clouding our ability to judge duration has to do with the length of time since the event occurred. Picture it this way. Every so often we go through a year that's overloaded with big changes: get a new job, have a baby, survive a tornado, leave old friends and move to a new city, deal with an illness, whatever. Life-altering events transpire at an unusually fast pace. Odds are that during that year you were so occupied that time seemed to race by, but months later, in hindsight, the year seemed unusually long. In the deadline scenario a few pages back, time flew as we struggled to hit the target, and we were shocked that so many days had passed when we were done. But a few months later, the block of time dedicated to completing that project may have felt longer than the five days it actually took.

Our friend Sebastian told us the following story, which illustrates some of the major factors that social psychologists say shape our perceptions of an event while it's happening. Sebastian, who is in his thirties, travels to Rio de Janeiro, Brazil, every six months for his job. Immigration and Customs are a familiar drill for him, but clearly not for some tourists. He told us about an incident involving a typical return flight arriving at Washington Dulles International Airport at 5:30 a.m. Several other international flights had arrived at around the same time, and the lines to clear Immigration held more than 300 people. Near him was a couple returning from vacation in Rio, their first trip abroad. He heard them immediately begin to fret about making their connection to Denver nearly four hours away. Sebastian tried to put their minds at ease by telling them that he made the trip every six months and that he always made an even tighter connection when the lines were as long as this one. The couple thanked him politely.

As the line inched along, Sebastian used his iPad to organize his notes about the trip. At 7 a.m. and with at least 100 people still ahead of them, security agents announced that those with connecting flights prior to 8:30 a.m. could move to the front of the line. Sebastian and the couple were subsequently relegated to the back. The couple began commenting on every delay in the process, noting everyone being questioned and counting every minute that ticked by. As Sebastian continued to work, he could hear their rising panic as they discussed their options. The husband even approached the agents, who sent him back to the line. Ultimately, everyone had cleared Customs and Immigration by 8:15 a.m., though the couple appeared frazzled and much the worse for wear as a relaxed Sebastian bid them a good journey home. They made their respective connections, as well—Sebastian on a 9 a.m. flight to Los Angeles and the couple on a 9:20 flight to Denver.

Obviously, Sebastian and the Denver couple experienced the same service encounter very differently. Social scientists would predict that they also perceived its duration differently while it was happening and differently in retrospect much later. Having been through this experience several times, Sebastian knew how the process would evolve. The couple, new to international travel, had no idea of how long Customs would take and whether or not the process would keep them from making their connection. Interruptions in the process by agents sending other travelers ahead in the queue exacerbated their anxiety. On top of that, no one likes ceding their place in line. Sebastian passed the time working on his report while the couple watched the clock. Absorbing activities pass faster than agitated ones. Also, negative emotional states dilate time. Sebastian's assessments at the time and in hindsight would be based on whether the duration was comparable to those of prior experiences and whether it was consistent with his expectations.

When the couple got home, they would vividly describe the harrowing experience to their friends. Their lack of familiarity with airport procedures and the novelty of the experience would make it memorable. They would probably describe it as lasting longer than Sebastian would. The interruption at 7 a.m. broke their painful wait into two segments. The number of distinguishable segments aids our ability to store and recall memories, which creates a perception of longer duration. Remember the pot watchers who were told to monitor details? Also, emotional memories endure.

From an organizational perspective, we conceive of time as a linear process occurring in regular increments. This perspective makes it possible to plan, and it works extremely well for organizing activities. Plainly, it does not accurately describe psychological time.

FACTORS THAT INFLUENCE DURATION JUDGMENTS

Following is a list of factors that influence our judgment of duration:

- **Emotional state.** Stronger emotions dilate time perceptions, negative emotions more so than positive emotions.

- **Number of distinguishable segments.** Events with more distinguishable segments seem longer. Segments aid our ability to store and recall memories, thereby creating a sense of longer duration.

- **Attention to the clock.** Paying attention to the passage of time makes time seem to drag.

- **Expectations as to length.** Events in excess of the expected duration time seem much longer than they actually are.

- **Familiarity with the event.** Novel events create new memories and seem different form the same event experienced many times.

- **Uncertainty.** Uncertainty or lack of knowledge as to the service process adds to anxiety and increases the perceived duration.

- **Evidence of progress.** Evidence of progress toward the goal diminishes anxiety about the wait in most services.

- **Engagement.** Customers who are otherwise engrossed or engaged pay less attention to the passage of time than those who are preoccupied with it.

- **Control over activities.** The more freedom customers have to move about and do other things, the less attention they pay to duration.

- **Information about the event and the wait time.** Knowing what will happen and when it will happen decreases the attention paid to time.

THE VALUE OF TIME

In order to design service experiences, we not only have to understand how we make subjective judgments of duration, but we also have to understand how we value time. Our general valuation of time is consistent with our intuition that time is a scarce resource. Time is different from money in that it is not fungible; there is nothing we can substitute for time. Time lost today cannot be recovered tomorrow—or ever. Consequently, we generally appraise the value of time as we would any finite or scarce resource, and yet that value varies according to our satisfaction with the activity on which we expend it. Since we plan activities based on their expected duration, the size of the block of time we allocate for a particular activity reflects the *marginal value* of time, marginal because its value to us is subject to change with conditions that may or may not be associated with the activity. We dislike uncertainty in time because it makes it difficult for us to plan.

FACTORS THAT ALTER YOUR CUSTOMERS' VALUATION OF TIME

There are some factors that affect and alter your customers' valuation of time. These include:

- **Deviations from expectations.** Deviations interfere with our plans, especially when activities take longer than expected, which then increases the value of the time they take.

- **Relative deviation.** On the other hand, waiting for 35 minutes when you expected to wait 30 is not nearly as bad as waiting 35 minutes when you expected it to be only 15 minutes.

- **Context and perspective.** In a purely rational world, all 5-minute increments would be valued equally if cost or price per minute remained constant. Just as saving $5 on a $20 purchase is a triumph but saving $5 on a $200 purchase is not, everyone knows that shaving 5 minutes off a 20-minute experience feels much better than shaving 5 minutes from a 2-hour experience.

- **Uncertainty.** Humans are risk-averse when it comes to time. We prefer a certain 30-minute wait to a wait that could last 15 minutes or 45 minutes.

- **Consolidation of pain.** Given a choice, most people prefer to get multiple waiting experiences over in one shot if possible. Suppose that you plan to buy tickets for a baseball game and to renew your driver's license. You know you'll wait an hour in one line and 45 minutes in the other. Most people would choose to accomplish both tasks on the same day.

- **Culture and age of the individual.** Highly regarded rituals place a high marginal value on the time they take. Attempts to "save" time by cutting such rituals short can have the opposite effect from the one sought. Marketing professor Robert Graham illustrated how culture can mitigate the time-is-money equation:

> Not long ago, many banks installed "snake lines" in their urban offices in an attempt to save time for their customers. With this concept, people were required to enter a single line and then move through the line in single file until they reached the head of the line, where they would be served by the next available teller. When one bank instituted this line in an urban branch that essentially serviced an ethnic community, the customers were outraged. It seems that many customers had established a ritual of going to the bank on certain days, talking with certain people, and being served by a certain teller. The idea of upsetting this process just to save time seemed outrageous—and it was, to them.[4]

- Incidentally, Graham's article further points out that Spanish speakers have a unique way of expressing their perception of time:

> The Spanish language has a past, present, and future tense, but time is spoken of in a manner different from the Anglos. In English a clock runs, while in Spanish it walks (*el reloj anda*). In addition, the passage of time to the point of being late for an appointment is viewed as almost independent of the actions of the individual. A late arrival would not say, "I am late," but rather, "It got late on me."[5]

PACING AND CULTURAL INTELLIGENCE

Cultures across the globe differ significantly regarding the appropriate pace for different types of events and interactions and even life itself. With the cultural variations in pace come cultural variations in duration as well. Successful multinationals train their employees in *cultural intelligence*, meaning they teach them to interpret and respond effectively to people representing diverse nationalities, backgrounds, personalities, and capabilities.

A senior executive for Dell in Europe told us about the different expectations that people in Europe and the Middle East have for the pace of conversations with call center agents. She said that customers in Europe tend to focus on the core aspects of the task and prefer short calls. Customers in the Middle East, however, expect the service agent to engage in polite conversation and want to exercise more control over the pace and direction of the conversation.

The rhythm and pace of restaurant meals in the United States stand in stark contrast to those in Asia and Latin America. In China, it would be considered rude for a server in a restaurant to present a bill or even ask if a customer is ready for it; both actions would be considered pressure. Instead, the server is expected to wait politely until the patron requests the bill. A typical restaurant meal in China, however, doesn't run as long as one in Spain and Argentina, where restaurant patrons spend what seems like endless hours over their lunch or dinner. In these countries, the customer completely controls the duration of the service encounter. Most eating places in the United States measure success by their table turnover rate and train their staff to keep the process moving.

Age actually presents what might be considered cultural implications for pacing. According to the extensive literature on temporal perspective, we shorten our outlook as we get older. Thus elderly people tend to live in the present and think less about the future. The not surprising implication of this is that service actions and outcomes for seniors have to be clearly specified.

Customs and border protection service may never take steps to improve or even care about the experience of international travelers passing through Immigration and Customs. We can learn from Sebastian's tale, however, and apply what we know about the factors that affect our sense of elapsed time and its value. We're ready to leverage those insights into actions that reduce the pain of the wait, build the pleasure of anticipation, and even help the customer enjoy the interaction.

REDUCING YOUR CUSTOMERS' PERCEIVED DURATION OF THE WAIT

The emotional content of the service determines whether consumers want wait times to be reduced in reality or in perception, as is the case with other aspects of service design. For emotionally neutral, utilitarian services, such as bank transactions, online trading, haircuts, grocery purchases, and ordinary restaurant meals, customers want brief waits. Customers also want short waits for painful or unpleasant services, such as dental emergencies, stock sales during a market decline, and flu shots.

Table 6.1 Value-added time in selected processes

Industry	Process	Average Cycle Time	Value-Added Time	Percent of Value-Added Time
Life insurance	New policy application	72 hrs.	7 min.	0.16%
Consumer packaging	New graphic design	18 days	2 hrs.	0.14%
Footwear	Prototype development	25 wks.	2 days	1.60%
Commercial bank	Consumer loan	24 hrs.	34 min.	2.36%

Source: Joseph Blackburn, "Time-Based Competition: White Collar Work," *Business Horizons* 35 (4), July–August 1992, 96–101.

According to customer service folklore, each American spends close to 6,000 hours waiting in lines over the course of a lifetime. In his research into organizations that speed up response times to gain a competitive advantage, Joseph Blackburn identified a range of services in which the value-added (human interaction) time constituted a very small proportion of the total processing time for a customer service request (see Table 6.1).[6] The customer spends essentially all the non-value-added time in a seemingly ever-elongating time warp—waiting for decisions, paperwork, approvals, information, schedule arrangements, or deliveries. Monopoly industries like the government passport office or the water company may not be very concerned about customer wait times because they have no time-based competition. For others, the dearth of value-added time plays right into the hands of the competition. It's a particularly acute problem associated with healthcare everywhere in the world, and it can be fatal. A widely held belief in global health is that more patients die on gurneys waiting for service than in hospital beds.

The best advice for firms providing utilitarian services is to aggressively reengineer their processes to reduce actual wait times.

George Stalk and Thomas Hout provide compelling examples of how this can be done and the resulting value to firms.[7]

For customers, healthy and otherwise, waits are the event-before-the-event or the value-added activity, as well as the event-between-events. For example, a visit to a primary care physician entails a minimum of four waiting periods, more if tests are involved. The first wait is for the day of the appointment, next is the wait at the reception desk to check in, then there's time spent in the waiting area, and finally, there's the wait in the exam room for the physician. While system dynamics and the economics of providing services make it impossible to eliminate waits, management should be aware of six design variables that can be manipulated to influence the perceived duration of waits and thus reduce the unpleasantness of the wait.

1. Monitor Wait Lines

We want the wait to be equitable. Even if it's just in our thoughts, we send our darkest maledictions to people who jump ahead of us in line. It doesn't matter if they have legitimately been given special priority for reasons unknown to us; they're perceived as insolent scofflaws. Everyone who uses a car ferry can describe a near riot erupting when someone cuts in line; Prius-driving commuters turn into raging peasants with torches. The law of the queue must prevail.[8]

We are angered not only because the jerk who jumps the queue moves those of us who play by the rules farther away from the goal, but also because it increases our uncertainty about how much longer we now have to wait. If this weren't bad enough, strong evidence indicates that negative emotions such as stress and anger worsen our existing predilection to overestimate wait times. There are several ways to ensure that the line is controlled:

- Install physical barriers to protect customers' places in line, such as at stadium entrances.

- Assign personnel to maintain line order such as marshals on the golf course, though perhaps their main responsibility is to move slow players through the course.

- Place a ticket dispenser near the door, and have customers take a number.

- Install monitoring technology like the automatic cameras at metered freeway on-ramps that photograph single drivers who illegally use the carpool lane to avoid waiting their turn.

Along with monitoring the line, standing customers require some additional considerations. Each person needs a minimum of seven, preferably ten, square feet of space. Studies have shown that small waiting spaces lead to more customers balking at entering the queue but fewer customers reneging (abandoning the line) after a few minutes.[9] When lines are long or the waiting people need to be confined to a particular area, movable queue barriers help maintain crowd control and impart a certain customer peace of mind as to expected duration. Also, establish a telephone answering protocol that gives priority to the customers who made the trek to the service facility and are already waiting.

2. Segment Wait Lines

Making waits equitable does not mean that all customers must wait the same amount of time. Supermarket customers expect to see express lanes for people buying only one or two items, and they accept them as fair. The willingness to wait with a full grocery cart positively influences our perception of time. That willingness varies according to the waiting person's expectations, emotional state, and regard for the service. Those who have been identified as high-value customers of financial services, airlines, casinos, and hotels expect to wait less than other customers. A person who is dealing with a service failure is not in a pleasant state of mind and is not willing to wait. When a call center hands off a customer to a higher level of support to address the same problem, the customer should not have to repeat the waiting process. In all these cases, service providers need to establish mechanisms for granting accelerated access, and all affected customers need to understand the rationale for the differences in waiting times.

3. Create Offline Waits

The highly competitive restaurant world has instituted many innovations for easing the wait time for customers. Restaurants like the successful Cheesecake Factory chain hand out pagers, which give patrons control over their choice of activities while they wait for their table. Service providers that deal with customers in person and are unable to convert all waits to offline waits need to make an effort to minimize in-line waits. Customers need to feel physically, or at least mentally, free from the act of waiting, hence the busy cocktail lounge located near the restaurant host's station. At least offer comfortable seating for texting.

A number of smartphone apps are available for estimating local restaurant waiting times so that customers know before they arrive what sort of wait time they can expect. Better yet, major league baseball provides a smartphone app called At the Ballpark, which includes concession food orders at many stadiums. Arizona Diamondbacks fans can place orders on their smartphones and pick them up when a text message arrives saying that the food is ready.

Reservation systems help keep waits offline. The Disneyland FASTPASS is a good example. Rather than shuffle through endless hot, snaking lines for a popular attraction, guests can insert their admission tickets in the FASTPASS machine located at the entrance to the ride. The machine dispenses a special FASTPASS ticket stamped with a return time range. When the guest comes back inside that window of time and shows the ticket to the "cast member" running the ride, the guest goes right in. Besides keeping the customer happy, The Walt Disney Company reaps a considerable side benefit from the money that freely roaming guests spend at its concessions.

Callbacks and take-a-number systems also keep the wait offline. Some call centers present a window inside which they promise to call the customer back, or they give the caller a selection of times from which to choose. A number of large call centers offer guaranteed callback options without delaying those who are willing to wait.

Even simple mechanisms such as take-a-number systems are better than in-line waits because they allow the customers to wander as long as they stay within earshot.

Primary healthcare has accepted an interesting trade-off from insurance companies regarding in-line and offline waits. By increasing the number of patients seen in a day, a physician can decrease the number of days a patient has to wait to get an appointment. On the other hand, visit times have been shortened. If the pressure to see even more patients per day increases, the likelihood of waiting in the physician's office will likely increase as well.

4. Keep Customers Informed

Updates regarding customers' positions in line or amount of time they can expect to wait gives patrons some sense of control. Often just having somebody to answer questions such as "Are we in the right place for the shuttle to terminal C?" is reassuring. Though some customers might balk at the information and choose not to get in the line in the first place, those who do enter tend to tolerate the wait as long as the estimate they received is accurate. The type of queue, visible or invisible, also makes a difference. The greater uncertainty created by an invisible queue, such as ringing a call center or waiting on hold, increases the importance of keeping the customer informed.

A quick glance at Figure 6.1, which shows how customers feel when they enter visible and invisible queues, reveals two progressions moving in opposite directions.[10] In the visible bank line, they're concerned at first upon seeing the length of the line, they become unhappy as they wait, they ease into a more relaxed frame of mind as they get nearer to the teller, and, finally, they're happy when they are being served. In an invisible phone queue, callers are optimistic when they place the call, indifferent while they begin the wait, increasingly unhappy as they are kept on hold, and decidedly unhappy by the time they reach the service rep because they waited what seems like an interminable amount of time.

Visible Queue: Bank

Invisible Queue: Phone

Figure 6.1 Visible versus invisible lines

Queue lengths aren't the only type of information that customers in visible queues use to estimate the wait duration. They
size up employee behavior, other customers, and the location.
Some institutions have learned to capitalize on some of these
other data:

- **RFID wait time tracking.** Often it's not just the primary person
  receiving the service who needs to be informed about progress.
  Most hospitals do a terrible job of letting patients' relatives and
  friends know what's happening. It's as if patients disappear
  onto a factory assembly line from which family and friends
  are completely shunted aside. One notable exception is White
  Memorial Hospital in Los Angeles, which tracks patients with
  RFID (radio frequency identification) tags. Admission staff
  members use this information to estimate wait times and keep
  the patients and their loved ones informed.

- **Number of persons behind.** Interestingly, progress can also
  be determined by the number of people waiting behind you.
  In fact, research shows that the number of people waiting

behind you in line influences reneging behavior (leaving the line). According to their research on queues at ATMs and post offices, Zhou and Soman concluded that, "The number behind matters because consumers tend to make downward social comparisons with the less fortunate people behind them in the queue."[11] They observed that the number of people behind exercises an ever greater influence on the decision to abandon the line when the line is linear so that a person's relative position is significant and inspires social comparison, if the individual is the sort of person who tends to make such comparisons (and who truly doesn't?).

- **Good timing.** Sometimes a person arrives in line just before a rush of other customers, a situational factor that Zhou and Soman say is likely to prompt people to flights of fantasy that contribute to feelings of superiority to those behind them. Consider the number of times you've heard someone say, "It was meant to be," one of the more hackneyed responses to good fortune. Even with hundreds of people in front, those hearty souls who camp in front of an Apple Store days before the latest iPhone goes on sale seldom renege. They relish the joy of beating everyone else to acquire the cool device. Beating the rush magnifies the downward comparison process and enhances the effect of the number of people behind.

Although the wait estimation examples deal with visible queues, there are also implications for invisible queues. Call centers might find that they are able to reduce the number of customers who hang up (renege) by informing them about the number of calls behind them, perhaps as cautionary advice.

5. Show Progress Toward the Goal

Making progress toward a goal mitigates the tedium of waiting. Signs of changed status trigger feelings—elation at progress toward the objective and frustration at stagnation or regression. Clearly, it is important to provide customers with a constant sense of progress. As with updates, customers tune in to a variety of indicators of progress in addition to the rate at which they shuffle forward in line. For example:

- **Number of segments**. In some situations, distinct segments impart an impression of progress. As we mentioned earlier, however, the number of waiting segments affects our sense of time passing, which is particularly treacherous territory for invisible waits. For example, two telephone waits of 10 minutes and 5 minutes seem longer than one wait of 15 minutes. Segmentation can work, however, when applied cleverly:

  - At a clinic, moving a patient from examination room to X-ray room and back creates a sense of progress, although clinicians need to be alert to expressions of pain, confusion, or a rising sense of fear.

  - At Universal Studios Hollywood, the waiting line for "Transformers: The Ride-3D" meanders through a half-dozen rooms, each of which contains videos and interactive elements that contribute to a different part of the backstory for the movie on which the attraction is based.

  - At the gym, built-in programs on the elliptical trainer break a 30-minute workout into multiple segments of variable intensity. This establishes a sense of progress.

- **Number of channels**. Perceptions of waiting time are affected by the number of channels into which an organization distributes the line of customers. Studies show that a single T-line, whereby one line feeds several service windows, is perceived as fastest when the service is fast—under two minutes. When service is slow, separating the line into two or more separate channels seems to customers to be a faster arrangement. This perception holds true even when the service times are exactly the same. A nimble arrangement for opening and closing channels would seem to be the best way to manipulate customer perception, allowing a provider to create multiple channels when service is taking longer than usual, regardless of whether or not it really speeds things up.

Instead, perhaps customers can be educated, as we describe later in the section "The Usual Grind," when we discuss ways Whole Foods Markets introduced value-added activities to the checkout line. A quick reality check shows that a single line going to three stations is faster than one line for each station. The reason is that each line in a multichannel arrangement could contain random line stoppers that require price checks or special assistance that could affect all in that line. In a single-channel line, the shopper behind a line stopper is not affected because other registers are quickly available.

- **Presentation of time**. How we present the passage of time has been shown to affect the way in which we gauge the length of delays. An experiment by DiClemente and Hantula examined our sensitivity to time when we receive feedback about its passage when we're shopping online.[12] The experiment compared three conditions for three groups of subjects buying CDs who saw either an ascending clock onscreen displaying the amount of time elapsing, a descending clock onscreen counting down, or, as a control, no clock onscreen. Participants showed greater sensitivity to delays in online shopping when the ascending clock cued them as to the mounting total time.

6. Provide Distractions

Although offline waits themselves go far to mollify restless customers, they may not be enough as we mentioned when we recalled restaurant cocktail lounges and comfortable seating. Some venues try to make the waiting experience so involving that time spent waiting is not viewed as an issue. They encourage patrons to engage in such activities as working, reading, socializing, shopping, or being entertained. Some even involve the customer in implementing the service. For example:

- **Let me entertain you.** Customers who are engaged in mentally absorbing activities are less likely to notice time passing and may actually underestimate the waiting time. Harvard Business School professor Stefan Thomke examined Bank of America experiments in customer service and reported that entertaining customers in the "transaction zone" by placing television monitors above the teller lines reduced the customers' perception of the length of the wait by at least 15 percent.[13] Expanding on the scenario, MIT professor Richard Larson, a waiting lines expert, says that giving the customer meaningful information, such as a stock ticker, encourages the customer to focus on the passage of time rather than irrelevant, lighthearted entertainment.[14] Some medical clinics provide self-testing devices such as thermometers, blood pressure cuffs, and breathing monitors for patients to play with while they are waiting for their turn to see the doctor. (Verifying Larson's nuance, one of the authors of this book admits that, while waiting to pick up prescriptions, he entertains himself with tabloid rags he grabs off the pharmacy magazine rack.)

- **Nobody expects the comfy chair** (apologies to Monty Python). Just having a pleasant place to wait is often the best way to manage a wait. The easiest customers to handle can be those who are instantly absorbed by their smartphones when they encounter a lull in the day. Airline traveler lounges are a cherished perk of road warriors whose frequent flying on a particular carrier qualifies them for a $300 to $500 annual membership. Each lounge is different, but they all provide a classy, comfortable, and quiet place to wait for a flight. They all offer free food and drink, entertainment, and travel assistance. Incheon International Airport in Seoul, South Korea, rated best in the world in 2012, gives international travelers

free access to sleeping chairs, showers, movies and television, live music, and online workstations. This is not to mention low-cost amenities like massage services, gym facilities, a golf course, and the Korean Culture Museum.

- **Help us out here.** Having the customer do some of the work makes the time pass more quickly for the customer and frees up servers. Most banks have elevated counters near the teller lines so that people can do paperwork—endorse checks, complete deposit slips, and so on—while they advance to the front of the line. At Wendy's fast-food restaurants, customers move their own trays through the ordering, paying, and food collecting process. If the service involves supplying data verbally or filling out forms, try to work it into the wait.

- **Join the crowd.** Customers can distract one another very effectively if the circumstances facilitate social interaction, including the time-honored misery-loves-company conversation about the slow line. Waiting by yourself feels longer than waiting with a group, especially when the service is anticipated to be unpleasant such as a dental procedure or legal deposition. Perhaps contrary to expectation, some waiting rooms, such as those in gynecologist and obstetrician offices, are more satisfactorily arranged with comfortable seats at angles to or facing one another to promote conversation rather than solitude. Restaurants have long recognized the role of bars in changing the nature of the wait.

- **Train to impress.** All front-facing employees, those encountered one way or another by patrons, personify the company brand. The impression they make affects the quality of the waiting experience. When staff members acknowledge customers or introduce customers to one another in a business waiting room, they also let the customers know that they are not forgotten, thus suggesting that the wait will be limited. Disneyland calls all its park employees—entertainers and

groundskeepers alike—cast members, identifying them as actors collaborating in a grand production designed to delight the perspiring dad and mollify the shrieking toddler weary of the line at the Buzz Lightyear Astro Blaster Ride.

The best companies also understand that customer service employees who are not actually serving customers should remain out of sight or switch tasks and start serving. There is nothing more irritating for an impatient bank patron than to watch a teller doing paperwork at a closed station while the line of people builds up. Then there's the department store clerk standing around, refolding shirts when a line forms at the cash register. The shirts can wait.

BUILD YOUR CUSTOMERS' ANTICIPATION FOR POSITIVE OUTCOMES

Companies can learn to enhance anticipation. Many different types of services have reaped the benefits of turning a wait into a period of mounting expectations. Certainly, when the service is merely utilitarian or expected to be negative, focusing on the duration of the wait clearly exacerbates the service experience. In such situations, distraction from the wait is the ticket. But these tactics can also be used to build anticipation for enjoyable services. Starbucks saturates your senses with a mellow, coffee-scented world, adding pleasure to the wait in line. The Transformers attraction at Universal Studios Hollywood incrementally builds the story as you proceed in line through each room; it also ratchets up the anticipation.

Connecticut supermarket chain Stew Leonard's does nearly $400 million in business at four supermarkets. For the company's 2,000 fortunate employees, *Fortune* magazine named it among the 100 Best Companies to Work For. As for customer service, the three-ton rock at each store entrance spells it out, "Rule 1: The customer is always right! Rule 2: If the customer is ever wrong, re-read Rule 1." Stew Leonard's maintains its own dairy and stocks

high-quality groceries, but what Stew Leonard's has truly mastered is anticipation buildup. It's no surprise that the founder idolized Walt Disney with all the singing animatronic milk cartons, bananas, and cows; costumed employees handing out samples; and Clover the cow mooing when someone tugs the rope. One of the canniest innovations is the single serpentine path forcing shoppers to go through the entire 100,000 square foot store, and yet no one complains about duration or delay.

The best restaurant in the world three years running according to *Restaurant* magazine, Noma in Copenhagen, has discovered a way to use anticipation to capitalize on its prestige and obviate the financial loss of a no-show. Noma books up so fast that its online reservation site posts the date (currently one month hence) for which it will accept reservations for an identified month another three months out. When a party cancels or fails to appear for the reservation, chef Rene Redzepi tweets the news, and customers jump to exploit the opportunity.

Delayed gratification has long been associated with opting for a larger payoff in the future over a quick reward in the present. In a little experiment involving chocolates (see box), researchers found that the anticipation enhances the perceived experience.

Waiting to Eat Chocolate

Nowlis, Mandel, and McCabe handed out chocolate bars to one set of subjects, told each to eat the candy, and had each person rate the experience. They gave chocolate bars to another set of subjects, had these subjects set their candy aside, and asked them to complete a set of tasks. Thirty minutes later, members of the second group ate the chocolate and rated the experience. Guess who enjoyed the chocolate most? Yep, the group that performed the tasks and then ate it rated the experience significantly better than the first group did.[15]

Creating anticipation can also create value for the service providers, something professional sports have mastered. The two-week gap between the last football playoff and the Super Bowl gives the NFL time to promote the matchup. College football has learned to do this just as effectively. The 2006 Rose Bowl Game between the University of Southern California and the University of Texas was a unique event in sports business, according to Tony Knopp, CEO of SpotlightTMS, a ticket management software company. That game may be the only one in which no tickets were available on any secondary market on the day of the game. One reason the demand for tickets was so heavy for the BCS National Championship Game is that all season long, the two teams were ranked first and second in the nation. Neither had been beaten in a year. Texas had won the Rose Bowl the year before and USC the year before that. For nearly two years, the excitement had built for a contest pitting one star quarterback against another. A few weeks before the game and with much hoopla, the USC quarterback won the Heisman Trophy with the UT quarterback coming in second. Sports commentators revved viewers nightly with superlatives and predictions. Participants followed the rules for creating anticipation about the upcoming event:

- Broadcast reminders

- Supply regular, vivid cues

We are hard-pressed to find other types of service providers that have learned to leverage their brand to build anticipation by going beyond mass media advertisements. We believe that there is an opportunity for many industries, including restaurants, tourism, entertainment, and leisure, to build customer anticipation.

ENHANCE VALUE-ADDED ACTIVITIES

The final key to managing customer perceptions of duration concerns the value-added component—the interactions and events contained in a service encounter. Aside from waiting in line for an event to begin, entertainment and other positive services themselves need to be so engaging that customers aren't paying attention to the time, and the duration of the value-added experience is not a major factor. We covered this idea in Chapter 5 with sequence theory, showing that as long as the actual duration remains consistent with industry norms, the peak-end rule dominates perceptions.

In our daily grind, packed as it is with emotionally neutral transactions of low consequence, such as checking out at the grocery store or getting telephone support for unfreezing the computer desktop, we want speedy service. The only caveat here would be that the pace of the encounter would have to be culturally appropriate in order to avoid conveying the impression that the server is in a hurry. We also don't want to wait long for the encounter itself. Theme parks entertain patrons zigzagging through the long queues, but augmenting the wait with value-added activities is none too common in day-to-day service encounters.

High-Value Service Encounters

Regarding professional services, the higher the value the customer places on the service encounter and the more interest the customer senses from the provider, the longer the desired duration of the interaction. In healthcare, the length of a medical appointment plays a significant role in patient satisfaction. Therefore, even if a patient waits a considerable amount of time for the appointment, the doctor visit itself should not seem hurried. Of course, there are trade-offs between extending the duration of a high-value interaction and the impact on waiting times or queue lengths, with longer service creating longer waits. Again, sequence theory indicates that when a service is considered worth the wait, prolonged delays are likely to be forgiven and forgotten.

In some situations, efforts are being made to actually prolong the duration of the service encounter or perceptions about it. The modern workplace increasingly emphasizes getting things done faster and still responding almost instantly to e-mails and text messages. If our work life is all about speed, the unhurried moments in our private lives become more precious and valuable. Slow Cities (now called Cittaslow) is an international organization of cities with populations under 50,000 that developed from Italy's 1989 "slow food" movement. Having begun as a protest against a surging global fast-food culture and an effort to preserve traditional regional cuisine, members of Cittaslow are committed to improving the quality of urban life, starting with slowing the pace of restaurant meals. Some member towns have gone so far as to slow traffic, ban car alarms, regulate cell phone use, preserve old buildings, and restore natural settings. In situations where there is value in dilating the perceived duration, breaking up encounters into multiple segments can make an experience seem longer and may add value to it as well. For example, during a Mediterranean Sea cruise, the ship's first officer might announce that, "You have just sailed past the third country on your one-week cruise from Naples."

In case the service encounter is not sufficiently high value, then augmenting the length of the interaction may mean that you have to introduce value-added activities during the wait.

The Usual Grind

Conferring with the waiter at a fancy restaurant, our friend Sebastian's note-sorting work in the Customs line, sipping a drink in a restaurant cocktail lounge, pushing your tray at Wendy's, completing a deposit slip—all constitute value-added activities that enhance the waiting component of a routine service encounter, though the customers created these themselves. Visible waiting lines are definitely the easiest type to augment.

When it comes to grocery shopping, the trip through the store is the fun part, especially at Stew Leonard's where customers look forward to each segment. However, checkout can be frustrating. The ice cream is melting, and we picked the slow line. This happens particularly often in Manhattan, where droves of shoppers pack supermarkets after work. Whole Foods analyzed the problem and went against tradition to institute a single line, snaking along to a huge bank of cash registers. Since customers favor multiple channels when the wait is more than a couple of minutes, Whole Foods provides a genial "traffic cop," or line manager, to monitor the line, direct shoppers to open registers, hold up signs indicating the length of the wait, and engaging the customers—all value-added activities. The customer response has been enthusiastic, and a 50-person line takes about four minutes to clear. Besides the line manager, the essential component is the number of registers, 30 in those Manhattan stores.

Other retailers have introduced value-added activities into the checkout line. Many stores that have switched to the single-channel T-line now position shelves of impulse purchase items along the route. When lines are long at Disney Stores or Home Depot, a queue buster steps forward to prescan the items, linking them to the buyer by scanning the buyer's customer loyalty card or a temporary unique ID and then relaying the data to the point-of-sale system up front. The Apple Store, where people wander around playing with equipment before they buy, gives floor sales staff handheld devices for ringing up purchases anywhere in the store. Closing the deal while the customer is still holding the dazzling mobile device leaves less time for reconsidering the investment.

CONCLUSION

Duration management is the complement to sequence theory discussed in the previous chapter. Optimal service designs take advantage of the psychology that underlies how we perceive events—their peaks and valleys and trends—and how we perceive the time between them. The goal is to frame service encounters so that "good time" in the system is remembered and "bad time" is forgotten:

1. **The service employee job should be viewed as time management for the customer.** The value of a service to a customer is hard to separate from the time spent waiting for it. And, like it or not, the server is the one who is traditionally seen as in charge of service time.

2. **"My time may not be your time."** Different cultures value time differently.

3. **Provide acceptable (to the customer) ways of changing queue priorities.** People accept the fact that first-class passengers get on the plane first and get served first. (It is a good idea to keep the drapes between first class and second class closed.)

4. **The waiting room is part of the service experience.** You can't make the hospital visit fun, but you can at least have Wi-Fi available for patients' visitors in the waiting area.

5. **Build anticipation of positive services.** Anticipation is the positive side of waiting. Watch your kids around Christmastime savor the prospect of a visit by Santa.

ATTRIBUTION: ENSURING THAT YOU GET YOUR DUE

I never blame myself when I'm not hitting. I just blame the bat, and if it keeps up, I change bats. After all, if I know it isn't my fault that I'm not hitting, how can I get mad at myself?

—Yogi Berra

Once a service encounter is completed and the dust has settled, we may look back and praise someone for a job well done, or we may find fault. Worse yet, we may file a lawsuit. The decision rides on the intensity of our residual feelings, the importance we give the matter at stake, and the party to whom we attribute the blame or credit. It's in the very nature of service encounters that expectations about satisfaction (or the lack thereof) prompt the customer to reflect on events and make attributions about the outcomes.

When things simply go as planned, we rarely think about the causes. If they go very well or very poorly, however, we're inclined to seek reasons. For instance, we're likely to attribute an exceptionally pleasant hotel stay either to a specific staff member or to the overall management of the facility. We're also likely to blame the investment broker who recommended stocks that underperformed. When a service encounter generates an emotional charge because of unexpected events or high stakes, we are all tempted to look back and indulge in a little "what if" speculation.

SUBJECTIVE PERCEPTIONS

While customers often assign credit or blame appropriately, there are many situations in which this is not the case. Anyone whoever taught or took a class knows it's a common tendency for students who do well to take full credit for being bright and talented and for students who do poorly to blame the professor for being uninspiring or giving outrageously difficult tests. Customers and service providers frequently disagree as to who is responsible for an outcome. For that matter, they often disagree as to whether the outcome was even a success or a failure. For example, when a knee surgery does not completely restore mobility, the patient might reasonably ask if it was failure while the surgeon might just as reasonably describe the partial restoration of a severely damaged joint as a success. Similarly, you might be thrilled with your new house until you learn a month later that a similar house a few blocks away was also for sale and provided a much better view. It makes you wonder why the real estate agent didn't show you that house.

Clearly, attribution disputes can arise from a subjective perception of error based entirely on each party's perspective. Professional services like healthcare, finance, and management consulting can produce ambiguous or uncertain outcomes. Furthermore, the actions of both parties contribute to those outcomes. The time it takes to heal from knee surgery and the extent of recovery that one can expect are greatly influenced by the patient's diligent participation in the postoperative rehab process. But, certainly, many other variables contribute to the outcome as well. Disappointing outcomes and defensive service providers can leave unhappy customers wondering how complex issues might have been handled more satisfactorily and wanting someone to take responsibility for the disappointment.

As we said earlier, instead of focusing on ways to deal with negative attribution, firms need to structure service delivery so as to minimize the likelihood of results that elicit negative customer reactions. Nevertheless, the same professional services producing uncertain outcomes also involve substantial risk, with the provider controlling only a portion of the variables. Throughout the 1990s, the business press routinely carried stories of large cost overruns incurred by firms implementing custom enterprise resource planning (ERP) systems, elaborate software applications that integrate data across all corporate business functions. The prospect of having all data relevant to decision making instantly available was so tantalizing that executives championed ERP projects despite their history of cost overruns and performance glitches. Several companies ended up in lawsuits.

The data standardization and security challenges of ERPs are similar to those presented by efforts to create electronic health record (EHR) software. The federal government stocked the 2009 stimulus package with incentives to develop EHRs and penalties to healthcare providers who have not adopted an EHR system by 2015, and yet, two years from the deadline, with incentives dropping off, implementation still lagged.[1] While 72 percent of office-based physicians were using an EHR as of 2012, only 40 percent of them said that their systems met the federal criteria for meaningful use. For all their promises to enhance efficiency and reduce errors, developing ambitious software systems like ERPs and EHRs entail complex technical standards, data synchronization difficulties, legal issues, and costs that are difficult to calculate. As early adopters of technology the world over can tell you, new technology is never bug-free. Although the errors and the risks usually decline over time—the notorious iPhone 5 map debacle notwithstanding—risk reduction is never the same as risk elimination.

Clearly, departments that plan service recovery and manage customer complaints need to understand how customers think and how they assign responsibility. Our obliging behavioral sciences again supply insights into the way we habitually explain—or spin—behavior and effects. By combining those insights with their theories and principles from earlier chapters, we can fully grasp and perhaps manipulate the rules of the blame game.

DO YOUR CUSTOMERS RECOGNIZE A SUCCESS OR A FAILURE?

The party who instigates the determination of success or failure makes the opening gambit in the blame game. And then both participants are set on the pathway from reflecting on the experience to ascribing blame or credit for it. We humans are contrary animals, though, and the path is not always obvious. In fact, unambiguously negative events can make us feel fortunate. Survivors of serious accidents typically describe themselves as lucky, in a sense perceiving a positive outcome. Imagine you are crossing a road and a car suddenly rockets past, missing you by inches. In addition to feeling terrified and outraged, you probably consider yourself lucky that you escaped being hit.

On the other hand, unambiguously positive outcomes can produce negative emotions, especially if the outcome was almost—but not quite—perfect. Suppose the seller accepts your first offer on the condominium you want. Instead of being thrilled, there's a reasonable chance that you instantly suspect that you could have offered less. Some lottery ticket buyers who miss the big jackpot by one number but still win a substantial payout consider themselves extremely unlucky. We see it during the Olympic games where silver medal (second place) winners tend to be less satisfied than bronze (third place) medalists, and the commentators inevitably reinforce that sense of failure.

We can also list a plethora of ambiguous outcomes in health-care, real estate, financial services, and education in which no one can objectively assert that the encounter truly could have turned out any better than it did. When an outcome generates strong emotions, we can always imagine a much worse or much better result along with a cause or a pathway to it. The ready availability of a cause or a means to an alternative outcome, however, is not an objective measure based on empirical evidence.

HOW YOUR CUSTOMERS MAY DISCERN THE CAUSE

When we sense that an extraordinary outcome has occurred, we are mentally capable of sifting through the evidence and logically determining true causes. When we attempt to engage in deliberate analysis, however, we remain vulnerable to a number of biases or subjective rules that limit our perspective—particularly when we are involved in the encounter—resulting in judgments that can lead us to the wrong conclusions. Consequently, we may wrongly attribute success or failure, and we may praise or blame the wrong party, largely because we wrongly delineated causes. Only one in five patients who potentially could file a medical malpractice lawsuit does so. At the same time, of those who do sue their physicians, many actually have not suffered a preventable medical injury. So we have one group that does not perceive a failure where one exists and another group that believes an uncontrollable outcome was actually controllable and therefore avoidable and denies the role of chance or shared responsibility. From a psychological perspective, discerning cause is often subject to the intriguing phenomena of *counterfactual reasoning* and *memory distortion*.

Counterfactual Reasoning

The wild card in attribution is the urge to engage in counterfactual reasoning, fantasies of events that did not happen but could have. Counterfactual reasoning is an important factor in service transactions, since so much of the service outcome is in the mind of the beholder. Consider the following illustration:

> Josephine delivered freight for a trucking company. Her usual route covered Malibu Hills, California. She almost always started at 8 a.m. A few times a year, she would stop at a local coffee shop. When she did so, her day started about 15 minutes later. It had been nearly four weeks since she last stopped for coffee, and on July 15 she decided to pay the shop a visit. At 8:14 a.m., she left the coffee shop and started up a canyon road to deliver a package to her first stop. At 8:35, she was navigating a narrow bend in the road when a red Porsche struck her truck head-on. Two days later, Josephine died of severe head trauma.

If you were asked to complete the sentence, "If only . . . ," how would you respond? The story draws our attention to Josephine's stop at the coffee shop and emphasizes the randomness of her patronage. Many people would jump to the conclusion that the accident could have been avoided if she hadn't gone there. They would also claim, just as illogically, that it doesn't mean they believe her visit to the coffee shop somehow caused the accident. The story shows the human drive to discern causality and illustrates the biased reasoning we are subject to, in this case subtly blaming the victim.

Our natural inclination is to search for a significant, clearly identifiable cause. We are uncomfortable with the idea that a confluence of minor events can cause a wholly unexpected outcome. We perform mental simulations, making specific substitutions to capture alternative scenarios: if only I had done x or y or z, things would have been different. Several assumptions stand out in this exercise:

- **The cause is discrete.** We assume that the cause is probably one thing (x, y, or z), rather than a continuous, intertwined series of events which in their totality determine success or failure. Josephine could have driven at a slightly different speed or spent a few more moments at the coffee shop.

- **Deviations are significant.** We fix on deviations from routines or norms as potential causes of unexpected results. It had been nearly four weeks, but on the fatal day, Josephine stopped at the coffee shop.

- **The last event takes priority.** We frequently overvalue the significance of the event immediately prior to the outcome, naming it as the cause. Think about a basketball player who misses his last two free throws when the points would have given his team the win; everybody forgets the earlier missed chances during the game.

- **Action is cause.** We are inclined to exaggerate the significance of human actions, preferring to interpret outcomes as consequences of human behavior instead of mere factors contributing to a larger system or environment.

- **"The fault, dear Brutus, is not in our stars . . ."** or **shoulda woulda coulda.** We cling to the belief that we are masters of our fates and that outcomes are always controllable. A corollary to action being cause, this assumption reassures us that we are in control.

We are bound to think about alternatives and explore causes when the outcome is significant and strong emotions are generated.

The more easily we think we could have changed events leading to the outcome, the stronger our feelings are and the more mental energy we expend in counterfactual reasoning. Near misses are notorious triggers of counterfactual thoughts. Near misses resulting in loss generate especially intense anguish and provoke exaggerated estimations of the ease with which disaster could have been averted. After watching those ferocious, perfectionist athletes on the U.S. women's gymnastics team at the Olympics for several days, you just knew that McKayla Maroney, heavily favored to win the vault, would clean the Russians' clocks. Instead, after having hit the mark 33 times in a row, she fell. Though she still took the silver, her sour facial expression on the podium suggested years of fantasizing about the myriad miniscule changes that should/would/could have brought about a different result.

Our feelings about the alternatives we imagine when we indulge in this mental simulation dictate the emotions we ultimately experience and the causes we identify. When the survivors of bad accidents consider alternative possibilities, they envision ways in which things could have turned out much worse, hence the feeling of good luck. For the person who just missed out on a lottery win, the alternative that looms largest is a big win, so misery ensues. And yet it's all relative. When implementing a CRM system generates 20 percent cost overruns, the chief information officer (CIO) will be less inclined to assess the project as a failure if the business press reports that a competitor experienced a 25 percent cost overrun. The rival's performance shifts the CIO's perspective and provides some consolation. It didn't change his expectation, though, and it's likely that he's annoyed that things didn't turn out better. Except when the near miss saves us, we almost always envision an alternative that is better than what transpired.

Memory Distortion

As with counterfactual reasoning, we mentally rehash events when an encounter generates emotions. Even when we reflect on an event immediately, memory comes into play. Eyewitness testimony, once the gold standard in criminal trials, is subject to many types of distortion, famously demonstrated by the 1999 invisible gorilla test.[2] Subjects were told to watch a video, ignoring the players in black shirts who were passing a basketball and counting the number of times players in white shirts passed a ball. Meanwhile, someone in a gorilla suit strolled through the scene. Half the subjects never even saw the gorilla. Meanwhile, the scientific certainty of properly performed DNA testing in criminal cases has caused many convictions based on eyewitness testimony to be set aside and has inspired many studies examining attention. Eyewitness studies have found several links between memory mistakes and attribution.

WHEN MEMORY PLAYS ATTRIBUTION TRICKS

Our recollections of past events don't simply fade. We are more likely to remember some aspects while other components of the experience may be forgotten or even modified.

- **Emotions select the details.** Our memories are selective; what we recall depends on the strength of our feelings about an event. When it is a pleasant or only moderately irritating experience, we are able to recall things quite accurately. When the event generates strong feelings, however, we pay close attention to a very narrow set of events or actors at the source and pay little attention to the surroundings. We recall the gist of what happened but recollect details poorly, though some of them were likely to be crucial in determining causes.

- **Interaction facilitates attribution.** The more the witness interacts with a person or setting, the quicker the witness can recall it and the easier it will be to attribute something to that person or place, even if neither played a role. If a patient always has the same doctor but different nurses during medical visits, then the patient is more likely to attribute outcomes to the doctor unless something out of the ordinary occurs to specifically draw attention to a particular nurse.

- **Repetition creates composites**. Businesses with high levels of repeat customers, such as retailers (online and brick and mortar), banks, hotels, and airlines, are interested in the way our memories get jumbled together and corrupt our outcome attributions. Consider your last two trips to the supermarket and try to distinguish them. We create mash-ups of repeat events into single composite memories when they actually occurred during different visits. We may accurately recall specific components but not precisely when they happened or who was involved.[3] In a research setting, subjects given the words "spaniel" and "varnish" to remember clearly recalled "Spanish" as having been one of them. To service providers, this sort of *memory conjunction error* means that different encounters you have with customers over time get lumped together in memory.

- **Memories fade**. Unless intense emotion sears a memory into our brains, however incomplete, recollections slowly fade, and attribution fades with them. We forget who came up with the great idea, whether the rep was a man or a woman, and where we went to celebrate a minor victory. The larger the amount of time between an event and analyzing a cause or attribution, the less likely the cause that is remembered will be correct.

- **Goals adjust the details**. Memories can be adjusted unconsciously to suit goals. Patients at weight-loss clinics sometimes overstate their original weight to demonstrate greater progress, whereas people avoiding diets are known to lowball their weight. Recently reformed caffeine junkies can be very self-righteous about having seen the light and may overstate their daily consumption, while coffee drinkers clinging to the habit may underestimate it.

- **Fondness colors the recollection**. Liking someone creates bias when it comes to recalling details because feelings intrude on their objective importance. If you like your tax accountant, you may recall in retrospect that she was especially thorough and accommodating.

- **Outcomes interfere with objectivity.** Unfortunately, negative events loom larger than positive events, and losses loom larger than gains. Thus negative outcomes prompt exaggerations of other negative aspects of an experience. Patients who respond poorly to a treatment they underwent often retrospectively recall greater anxiety before the treatment than they reported at the time.

. . . and So *Everything* Sucked

MBAs at the USC Marshall School of Business go on an international study trip at the end of the first year. Several years ago, two groups of students went to China; one to Shanghai and the other to Nanjing. Both groups flew on the same plane between Los Angeles and Shanghai. The group that went on to Nanjing had a much better experience than the group that stayed in Shanghai. Upon their return to Los Angeles, both groups were asked to rate all aspects of their visit, including the air travel. Even though both groups took the same flights to and from China, they provided significantly different evaluations. The unhappy Shanghai group offered numerous negative comments about the flight to Shanghai, while the Nanjing group had nothing critical to say.

HOW YOUR CUSTOMERS MAY ASSIGN RESPONSIBILITY

Almost always, customers subconsciously subject attributions to a bias that protects their self-image and self-esteem. Therefore, it isn't surprising that customers tend to credit themselves for service success and blame others for service failure. This doesn't mean that we never assign the blame to ourselves. In fact, we often blame ourselves when we are extremely distressed but lack an objective basis for self-recrimination. In particular, victims of trauma, violence, and tragedy show pronounced tendencies to blame themselves. The challenge to service providers with respect to assigning blame is to ensure that they get the credit when it is due and that customers share the blame as appropriate.

False-Consensus Effect

Along with counterfactual reasoning and memory distortion, we are also prone to a form of motivational bias called the *false-consensus effect*. Customers prefer to believe that others share their preferences and consumption habits, thus normalizing their own preferences and habits. Because common behaviors seem more appropriate and reasonable than unusual behaviors, we are liable to bolster our self-esteem by overestimating our similarity to other customers. Successful marketers know that they can't always project their taste onto a wider public—remember New Coke?—so they hold focus groups and perform surveys to test ideas.

When it comes to services, providers need to examine assumptions that seem to them to be simple common sense. A friend who survived breast cancer laughs about stunning her oncologist at her first chemo appointment by having a fit over the 20 pounds that patients tend to gain on that particular treatment regimen. The doctor hadn't told her about the likely weight gain, having assumed that her good prognosis far outweighed such trivial matters. The fact that she learned about the side effect elsewhere plunged her into a black hole of consumer dissatisfaction.

Hindsight Bias

Looking back over events after observing the outcome, we tend to weigh evidence that supported the outcome more heavily than evidence that pointed in other directions. *Hindsight bias* makes outcomes look more predictable than they really were. The bugaboo of historians and doctors, hindsight bias makes risks start looking like inevitabilities. The phenomenon has serious implications for expert testimony and retrospective judgments about risky decisions. A company biased by hindsight might blame a software development failure on the product manager who took input from many subject matter experts, considered the advice, but didn't select the one item from one person who happened to provide a warning about the type of failure that occurred.

The outcome also clouds our judgment about the very competence of the product manager and other decision makers in risky contexts. We overestimate competence when the outcome is favorable and underestimate it when the outcome is unfavorable, even when we know that the outcome was a gamble. The stockbroker who recommended that you buy Apple shares in 2006 is a genius. The ski instructor, however, is an incompetent boob, because you spent most of your time at Aspen on your derriere, though it was the resort brochure that rashly promised you would ski like a professional after three days.

The Stability Dimension of Cause

Customers judge whether the cause is stable—meaning permanent—and then assign blame or credit. Thus *stability* refers to whether we expect the cause of the event to change over time or under different circumstances. If a data services firm has always provided reliable service, then we're liable to disregard an unexpected website crash as an uncontrollable event and assign no responsibility for it to the firm. If we think the failure is likely to occur again, then we blame the organization.

The perception of stability contributes to our subjective interpretation of errors and incidents involving personal treatment. Let's say that you ordered a caffeine-free diet cola with a twist of lime, but the waitress forgot the lime. On the other hand, let's say that she filled the order correctly but behaved rudely. The two scenarios generate completely different reactions and attributions. A mistake in filling the order, a task error, is more easily forgiven and is generally not seen as a stable problem. After all, we make mistakes too. It could have happened with any customer as well, so the error is not seen as an act directed specifically at you. On the other hand, her rudeness was directed specifically at you, and it feels personal. It seems more like a character flaw than a lapse, which makes this a stable problem with the waitress. Whether or not you ultimately attribute her behavior to the restaurant depends, as we discussed regarding judgments of trust in Chapter 3, on whether you believe her behavior was characteristic of that culture (the restaurant).

FEELING THE HURT

Two factors significantly influence our reaction to our assessment of success or failure and assignment of credit or blame. We care whether an outcome results from action or inaction, like the so-called sins of commission or omission. It also matters whether an outcome was caused by lack of ability or lack of effort.

Action Versus Inaction

Customers care more when a negative outcome follows action than when it follows inaction. Suppose that you own stock in Ford Motor Company and Coca-Cola Bottling Co. Consolidated. Imagine that in January 2012, Ford stock was trading at $12 and that Coca-Cola was trading at $57. By the end of the year, Ford had dropped to $11.45 and Coca-Cola had climbed to $70. Consider how you'd feel at the end of the year if that previous January your financial advisor had advised you to:

- Sell your shares in Ford and buy shares in Coca-Cola, but you did *not* follow her advice

- Sell your shares in Coca-Cola and buy Ford, and you *did* follow her advice

The net economic effect on your portfolio might be the same, but most people would suffer greater regret with the second scenario. In other words, we're more upset when an action results in a poor outcome than when inaction results in a poor outcome. Likewise, we're much happier when an action results in a positive outcome than when inaction does. This is because of our tendency to view inaction as the norm and action as unusual. Action is also much more conspicuous than inaction.

Ability Versus Effort

Customers really hate it when lousy outcomes appear to result from lack of effort. Performance plays an important practical role in attribution, and when the execution is inadequate, the distinction between lack of effort and lack of ability is critical. When it's the result of lack of effort, customers are likely to be angrier than when the provider is trying to do the job but lacks the ability. Of course, since lack of ability is usually viewed as stable, service providers will lose customers if the customers conclude that the firm's workforce is incompetent. Lack of effort is considered unstable because this could change.

Ability (or capability) would also be considered stable, setting the bar for service encounters, and effort would still be necessary to maintain the standard over time. In the eyes of the customer, however, the provider's ability encompasses the level of competence at their first meeting as well as whatever the provider learns throughout their association. Since learning is subject to effort, it's clear that customers are drawn in by ability but retained by effort. Clients seek experienced attorneys with high levels of ability in a particular field because the attorneys should be able to provide a stable and controlled result throughout a case. If, however, the lawyer fails to make the effort to learn the specific details of the case, then the ability level means almost nothing. Even the best lawyers need to spend sufficient time taking depositions, learning the details, studying legal precedents, and drawing up incomprehensible but airtight documents. Those who fail to put in sufficient effort to control the outcome and provide a stable result will be judged as incompetent *and* find themselves confronted by outraged clients. Given that ability and effort are difficult to directly observe or quantify, either can quickly be seen as causes of outcomes, especially poor outcomes.

CHANNELING YOUR CUSTOMERS' ATTRIBUTION

Based on the insights provided into how we evaluate an event, discover causes, and assign blame or credit, we propose a set of strategies for channeling attribution.

Keep Expectations Conservative

Expectations provoke attribution. Customers tend to assign credit or blame when the service is better or worse than they expected. Since negative outcomes are even more likely to trigger judgments about performance than are positive ones, smart management promises too little rather than too much. (Scotty in the old *Star Trek* TV series responded to desperate orders from Kirk with, "I cannae change the laws of physics!" and then he would save the ship anyway and look brilliant.) Overpromising in IT consulting can be especially costly, manifesting as an increase in the scope of the project, which exaggerates expectations and opens the door to a multitude of errors that present themselves during product development rather than up front when requirements were defined.

Move Risky Activities Up in the Service Cycle

Especially in consulting, software, and construction projects, it's a good idea to undertake the activities that are likely to fail earlier rather than later in the cycle if you can. This makes economic sense and increases the available recovery time. It also minimizes the impact of counterfactual thinking, which focuses on events occurring at the end.

Allow Your Customers to Control More Processes and Decision Making

The level of control customers exercise over processes and decision making influences attribution. Self-service and active involvement in service activities change the customer's role from passive consumer to producer. Accordingly, the desire to save face (self-serving bias) inclines the consumer-cum-producer to acknowledge any uncontrollable events that negatively influenced the outcome. Even without bias, involvement in service production makes the process transparent, keeps all participants on the same page, and encourages customer objectivity in evaluating the cause of the problem.

Let's say that you're booking a flight online. The site shows you all available seats, and you have a strong preference for aisle seats. That day, many aisle seats are available, but you don't book the seat. A week later, you go back to the website and discover that no aisle seats are available, so you settle for a window seat. But suppose, instead, that you didn't have access to the Internet a week later, and you called an agent who told you the same thing: all he could do was to give you either a middle or window seat. Most people feel angrier at the agent than they would if they make the discovery themselves.

Inform Your Customers of Risks

When the firm makes a risky decision, the representative must properly communicate that risk to customers at the outset. The challenge here is to objectively lay out the risk and to clearly justify the decision. Overstating the positives at a decision point can create problems when there's a possible negative outcome. Restaurants that provide slightly conservative wait-time estimates save themselves considerable grief later from hungry, disgruntled diners.

Make the Effort and Concern for Your Customers' Welfare Evident

Customers who think their service provider slacked off or disregarded them are prospective, finger-pointing ex-customers. Clearly showing evidence that the firm has made a concerted, good-faith effort and effectively conveying the firm's commitment to their welfare reduces the customers' desire to ascribe blame. Medical malpractice data reveal that patients who believe their healthcare provider didn't care or had poor communication skills are the ones most likely to file lawsuits.

Pave the Path to Success

Delineating the steps to completion makes the process seem doable. Weight Watchers continually seeks individuals to present weight-loss testimonials and to lay out the steps they followed. Firsthand accounts vividly characterize the sort of person who succeeds in the program by way of customers that the audience can identify with. The effort works against self-serving biases by encouraging customers to take responsibility for failures.

Cannot Is Better Than Will Not

Customers don't always know what can or cannot be done, so the way you say no makes a difference. Their sense of what should be done may drive the service request, but their ultimate satisfaction is dictated by what can be done. As happy as they are when a rep bends a rule or makes an exception to help them out, they really get annoyed if they find out that the rep *chose* not to perform a task. They would much rather hear that the rep lacked the authority to do so. Moreover, satisfaction increases when the customer hears that industry norms, construction codes, or some other regulation prevents the provider from fulfilling the request.

Keep Near Misses to Yourself

The near-miss phenomenon associated with momentous events is a common feature of daily encounters as well. A ticket agent doesn't do the company any favors by saying to the sports enthusiast, "If you had called just a minute earlier, you could have purchased the last ticket." In a heartbeat, blame takes over and anger flares. Reps should never bring up the obvious fact that a customer needed to have called much earlier. A better response would be to say sympathetically, "I'm sorry but tickets have been sold out for quite a while." Thus the agent becomes the reluctant but supportive messenger rather than the nasty gatekeeper.

Customers view honest gestures of hope in a positive light, even when the outcome turns into a near miss. Innumerable anecdotes depict grateful patients thanking the medical professionals who sustained their hope in their darkest hour.[4] You encounter such gratitude in a wide range of services, such as when the airport shuttle driver promises to try to park next to the sidewalk baggage check because your luggage is so heavy. Even if the departure lanes turn out to be too crowded, you will thank him for trying.

List the Positive Outcomes You've Obtained and the Negative Ones You've Avoided

A sincere presentation of positive outcomes that accrued through an encounter and the possible negative events that were avoided can influence t he alternatives that customers use as a basis for counterfactual reasoning. Keep it completely honest if you want to sustain trust. Supermarket receipts now commonly integrate these components to show the savings on individual sale items and total savings at the end, thus associating every penny saved with an item (obtained) and the grand total saved (avoided).

Emphasize Your Customers' Role in Successful Outcomes

Service providers need to set their egos aside in order to reap the benefits of pointing out the customers' role in positive outcomes. By reinforcing customers' participation in the successful execution of the processes and decisions, you play off their self-serving bias and ignite positive feelings. Frontier Communications is a small-market telephone company out of Stamford, Connecticut, that also offers Internet and satellite television bundles. Phone conversations to resolve service issues always end with the service rep thanking the customer for helping her troubleshoot and resolve the problem, and the rep always calls back to see how it turned out.

Celebrate Success with Your Customers

Educational institutions do a wonderful job of celebrating student success. They are keenly aware of the alumni largesse to be reaped from mounting those moving graduation ceremonies that highlight student accomplishments and create an emotional and memorable platform for praising the institution. To that same end, firms can leverage the many social media—as if they were alumni associations—including fan pages and blogs, through which customers can wax eloquent regarding their positive experiences.

Adhere to Norms and Rituals

Counterfactual reasoning is prone to raise its ugly head when providers violate traditional norms and rituals customers expect in the service encounter. Adherence is particularly important in professional services—healthcare, management consulting, software, engineering, legal, financial—that are too complex for customers to verify precise outcomes and their causes. Instead, customers often form judgments about service quality from rituals for communication processes and procedures and from norms associated with dress, report format, and appointment scheduling. When this is the case, norms and rituals are functioning as surrogate scripts that dictate the behavior of both parties. And when something goes wrong, the customer will attribute the source of the error to minute deviations from the script.

There may be no business environment in which the customer is more sensitive to norms and, most especially, rituals than in casino gambling, where, of course, all the rituals revolve around luck, a key performance variable identified in Chapter 2. Check out Payton's Mojo [luck] Rules for playing craps.

Payton's Mojo Rules

1. When the dice go off the table, that is *very* bad. They have been tainted by the dirty floor that has been walked upon by losers, and all the positive energy has been drained out.

2. The next number up is a "7" when the waitress either brings you a drink or taps on your shoulder. This is because she wants money (a tip), so she drains the positive flow from the table and straight to her drink tray. Waitresses should be fast, silent, and proficient so as to not suck the life out of a good game. She'll get a tip when I'm drunk and rich.

3. If it's taking a *very* long time between rolls (e.g., people cashing in money, placing complicated or silly center table bets, or changing their minds), this is the *worst* sign of all. The more time that passes, the more bets are typically placed. It's like fattening up the hog before the slaughter.

4. Finally, the weird one. If the dice are coming *towards* me on the table, I must lean on my right leg. If the dice are going *away* from me, I must shift my weight to my left leg. This has always worked well for me and, if anything, has prevented back strain.[5]

While casinos have no control over what players select for their personal rules, Harrah's goes to great lengths to learn the rules that its particular high rollers follow and to instruct its staff members to be sensitive to them. Harrah's staff members also work to modify factors that are commonly perceived as interfering with good luck.

So rather than asking a gambler how his luck has been running, they ask if he's getting good service or if his room is comfortable. This minimizes the negative emotional response that might be directed toward the casino during a bad streak and emphasizes the casino's dedication to making the controllable part of the experience as pleasant as possible. In Payton's list, training waitresses to be "fast, silent, and proficient" and croupiers to subtly keep the game moving along contributes to a feeling that "the house is lucky."

Provide Reasonable Explanations

Explanations impart a feeling of mastery over one's domain and give customers something they can work with at each phase. For example, the best-managed call centers provide an explanation for every action before the conversation goes quiet while the agent looks up information or enters data.

Apologize or Compensate

Failures are the result of task errors (doing the job incorrectly) or treatment errors (being rude or discourteous). If employees are rude to the customers, a sincere apology is needed. Such treatment errors don't typically call for monetary compensation. On the other hand, task failures necessitate refunds or other forms of compensation as well as an apology. Apologies imply culpability, which may entail liability, a problem greatly feared by healthcare professionals. The University of Michigan Health System, however, instituted a full disclosure policy in 2001, which included apologies and compensation for harmful medical errors. To the institution's shock, liability claims *immediately declined* by nearly 40 percent and lawsuits by 65 percent.[6] Since then, many hospitals have implemented disclosure, apology, and offer programs modeled after the one in Michigan, including the hospitals and clinics at Stanford University, which has saved $3.2 million each year since the program began.[7]

As to negative outcomes occurring because of factors beyond the firm's control, a recent study at MIT's Sloan School of Management suggests that the best course of action is to sympathize with the customer and clearly identify the cause, but do not accept responsibility for the outcome.[8] The researchers studied different responses by a retailer to product stockouts. They found that the best option was not to offer a discount but to simply state that the item was extremely popular. That statement alone increased customer back-ordering and sustained customer loyalty.

Facilitate Customer Feedback

Customer complaints are not always handled in a credible manner, especially in mass customer businesses. Establishing simple channels for voicing complaints and then explaining how the complaint was handled can go a long way toward increasing customer loyalty. The advent of Facebook, Twitter, Yelp, TripAdvisor, electronic mail, and text messaging has dramatically altered the ability of customers to express their views. While these outlets give customers a voice, organizations still need to develop effective response mechanisms. One public health physician in Recanto das Emas, a suburb of Brasilia, Brazil, encourages her patients to post positive and negative observations on the clinic's Facebook page. Rather than just have it serve as an avenue for venting, however, she posts responses and also cites any changes she has made.

PRINCIPLES FOR MANAGING ATTRIBUTION

The following principles can be used to implement the strategies discussed in this chapter:

1. **Celebrate the customer's success.** This is the "*You* did it" factor. Educational institutions do a wonderful job of celebrating student success. The graduation ceremonies highlight the accomplishments of the students while creating an emotional

and memorable platform for the students to praise the institution. There is a good opportunity here for firms to leverage fan pages, blogs, and social media, where customers can memorialize their positive experiences.

2. **Emphasize the customer's role in your company's success.** This is the "*We* did it" factor. By pointing out customers' roles in a positive outcome, you can play off their self-serving bias and increase their positive feelings toward the organization.

3. **Personalize service delivery wherever possible.** You want to have customers know employees by name. This is good for linking the customer into the organization and for giving attribution for employees' good work to their managers.

4. **Make pathways to success evident.** Weight Watchers continually seeks individuals who provide testimonials not just on their loss of weight but on the steps they adhered to in achieving the desired result. This serves the important function of saying that "people who succeed had these characteristics." This also works against self-serving bias and influences customers to take responsibility for failures.

PUTTING THE CONCEPTS TO WORK

Once you make a decision, the universe conspires to make it happen.

—Ralph Waldo Emerson

It is self-evident that delivering great customer experiences requires a deep understanding of customers' needs. There are several examples, including Disneyland and Starbucks, in which the original service concept was the brainchild of an entrepreneur who instinctively understood the consumer. There are also innumerable examples of service organizations in which an exceptional operations manager intuitively understands how customers think and what they need. The rest of us, unfortunately, have to rely on more traditional approaches to uncovering customers' needs.

There are several well-tested market research techniques, such as focus groups, surveys, mystery shoppers, and gap analysis, that have served us well in uncovering new concepts or improvement opportunities. We are now witnessing the emergence of techniques for analyzing unstructured data from social media. There are great expectations for *big data*. Despite their sophistication, these research techniques are limited to what customers can articulate about their experiences or the choices they make from among existing services. This is a limitation because there are several psychological factors that shape our perceptions and recollections, but we are not aware of their influence. As a result customers may indicate a liking or a disliking for a service, but they may not be able to explain why they feel the way they do or the reasons they provide may not help managers in finding a fix or reproducing what works well. Uncovering these hidden heuristics and biases has been an active area of research for behavioral scientists. We have sifted through their findings and selected those that managers can employ to engineer experiences.

To review, customers' perceptions and recall depend on their experienced emotions, the level of trust they have in the organization, their perceived sense of control, and the sequence in which the experience evolves. Time is the axis along which an experience evolves, but our perception of time itself is convoluted. A deeper understanding of factors that shape emotions, trust, control, and duration perception provides a platform for innovating service delivery. For example, we all know that customers waiting for a delayed flight are frustrated. However, recognizing that the frustration is rooted in a sense of loss of control enables managers to develop different mechanisms for improving the waiting experience. Managers can increase perceived control by informing customers about how long they have to wait and what is being done to address the delay, providing periodic updates, and permitting customers to leave the immediate boarding area if they like. Creative managers can do much more. The central message here is that the psychological factors (ETCs) discussed in this book shape perceptions and can be influenced through service operations. Fortunately, there are innumerable ways in which managers can "operationalize" these factors. *Knowledge of these principles also enables us to enhance the traditional survey techniques.* Surveys, focus groups, and analysis of comments on social media can be focused on variables such as trust, need for control, and so on.

Each of the preceding chapters has focused on a different psychological variable. By now it should be obvious that these variables are strongly connected. For example, if you trust your plumber, then you are less anxious and you are willing to cede greater decision control to him. If you are angry, then the duration of a wait is going to seem longer. On the other hand, if the problem is resolved well, you may forget the wait. Moreover, the relative importance of the ETCs depends on the industry, the positioning of the firm in an industry, and different customer interactions within a firm. The initial trust in a real estate agent and an orthopedic surgeon at USC Keck School of Medicine will be different.

IDENTIFY THE RELEVANT PSYCHOLOGICAL FACTORS

Before restructuring the service experience, managers have to identify the psychological variables that matter most to their business or their segment of the business. Is it trust that drives your customers' business decisions, are customers unhappy with the waiting experience, is it a purely utilitarian service like depositing a check, or are you in the business of generating hedonic experiences at ski resorts? Do you want to mitigate negative emotions, or do you want to accentuate the positives? Are you finishing on a strong note? Are there seminal aspects of your experience that dominate what customers recall?

The role of the emotional content depends on whether the service is utilitarian (such as banking) or hedonic (such as a rock concert). As we have seen earlier (Figure 2.1) most services have a utilitarian and a hedonic content. Even in purely hedonic services, there is a fun or a fantasy element and a real element that is utilitarian—such as seating arrangements, waiting lines, and restrooms at a rock concert. For hedonic services, the goal of the fantasy component is to stimulate emotions—they may be positive or negative.

For the fantasy element of hedonic services, questions of interest would be:

- Are we creating the right emotions?

- Are the emotions sufficiently strong?

- Are customers sufficiently engaged?

These services also have to be concerned with negative emotions in the real aspects of the service:

- What are the potential sources of negative emotions?

- Which activities or process steps are likely to generate negative emotions?

Rock in Rio organizes rock events in many different cities including Rio de Janeiro, Lisbon, and Madrid. Events last from five to seven days. Customers are present at the venue for 13 hours, enjoying music, participating in street dances, and riding Ferris wheels. In addition to providing a great musical experience, Rock in Rio is also focused on ensuring that the real aspects of the concert are trouble-free. It has discovered that to avoid conflicts and fights among customers who are there for many hours, it should eliminate any source of irritation in its ancillary services. There is minimal waiting at the restrooms, the floor of the outdoor stadium is covered with artificial turf to minimize dust, alcohol is restricted to beer, there is adequate space in the sprawling venue for those who want to step away from the crowds, and food prices at the concession stands are only slightly higher than those outside the venue.

For utilitarian services such as healthcare and financial services, the key questions related to emotions would be:

- What are the sources of negative emotions?

- Can we anticipate them?

- How do we mitigate them?

- What are the emotional high points?

In a similar vein managers can inquire about the information needs and control needs that arise at various stages of their service processes:

- What are the information and control needs at different steps in our process?

- Are we offering the right choices?

- Do customers feel they have adequate control?

- Do customers differ in their need for control and information?

In healthcare these questions are particularly applicable. Patients are often confused and do not know what is going to happen nor do they know who is responsible for different decisions. Also their information needs evolve over time. The first day at the hospital is not the same as the second day. We need to link process flows and control needs, just as emotions were linked to process flows in emotionprints. Information needs also vary by patient and medical condition. Some patients want to know, while others would prefer to quietly rely on the care providers.

In order to assess whether customers lack trust, managers have to answer the following questions:

- Do our customers believe that we have the skills to serve their needs?

- Are we seen as being trustworthy?

- Do they perceive that there are many risks in our industry?

- What are the trust-creating moments?

Real estate agents have a difficult problem in developing trust. They are not perceived as being very trustworthy, and customers underestimate the risks involved in a real estate transaction. The agent has the delicate task of educating the customer about the risks, delineating the responsibilities of an agent, and winning the customer's business by conveying competence and being motivated to act in the best interests of the client. Some agents believe it helps their trade if customers venture off and discover some of the risks on their own. For example, let us say that a customer finds a house on the Internet and indicates an interest in buying it. The agent, however, knows that the house has easement problems that the website with pretty pictures fails to mention. An agent would find this situation a valuable teaching experience. Professions with low baseline trust can benefit from moments when the customer is vulnerable. These are opportunities for the service provider to establish trustworthiness.

To leverage the sequence effects, firms have to understand the role of the beginning and the ending. If the baseline trust is low as in the case of a real estate agent or if the customer is highly distressed as in some healthcare settings, the beginning is very important. There may be an opportunity to start slowly and build to a high finish. Questions related to the sequence effects include the following:

- What is the role of the front end?

- What is the high point of the experience?

- What is the low point of the experience?

- Is there an opportunity to change the order of events?

- Is there an opportunity to introduce a highlight?

Call center conversations can be restructured to ensure that they end on a high note. Many services such as real estate transactions and child birth typically end on a high note. However, it may not always be possible to restructure the flow of events. In these situations it will be useful to explore the possibility of improving the low point and the high point. If all the events in an experience are similar, then it may be worth creating a new event that will be the highlight, preferably at the end.

DEVELOP SERVICE EXPERIENCE IMPROVEMENT PROJECTS

Reengineering your service experiences, like other process improvement activities, can vary considerably in scope. Below we describe two projects. They are restricted in their scope and involve changing only a few elements of the service cycle, such as the online purchasing process and interactions between nurse and chronic care patients. The approach that Harrah's undertook to focus on luck, on the other hand, was more strategic and touched most aspects of the business.

The approach to conducting a service experience improvement project based on our ETCs principles is about the same as any other process improvement project (see sidebar, "Structure of Traditional Process Improvement Programs"), but there are some important philosophical as well as technical differences. The first major difference is that managers and customer service staff steeped in the importance of a customer-focused philosophy as a determinant of success often have a difficult time thinking in psychological engineering terms. Many are caught in what we call the *culture trap*: "We have a great customer-focused organization, so why should we change?" Getting to a strong service culture is no mean feat, especially considering the pressures to cut costs of serving customers. At the same time, the recommendations of psychologically based modifications are really the embodiment of "quality is free."

A second difference is that there is the need to train implementation teams in a new set of concepts and move away from the traditional approach of focusing on meeting and exceeding expectations.

This may lead to counterintuitive process structures. For instance, according to sequence theory the ending is more important than the beginning. However, from a sales perspective the beginning is all important.

Structure of Traditional Process Improvement Programs

Phases of an improvement project

1. Recognition of an improvement opportunity or need

2. Authorization to embark on an improvement project

3. Development of alternative solutions

4. Selection of one or more solutions

5. Authorization to implement a solution

6. Implementation

7. Monitoring of outcomes

Organizational structure to support process improvement

Entity	Composition	Rationale	Objective
Steering Committee	Cross-functional team: senior managers and technical staff with knowledge of operations	The team should combine different types of knowledge in order to determine for any project its strategic importance, operational feasibility, and financial attractiveness	Authorize projects by allocating the necessary resources and defining the outcome metrics. Monitor projects. Monitor outcomes.

Ad-hoc project teams	Cross-functional team created for each project	This team must have the skill sets and the authority to execute the project by combining knowledge about operations, technology, and other relevant functions	Develop solutions and implement them. Implementation may require additional permissions from the steering committee.

Identification of problems and solutions (push and pull of ideas)

Internal continuous thinking about potential changes that can be made is illustrated well by the Japanese concept of *Kaizen*. *Kaizen* expects continuous improvements sourced from all levels within a firm. Organizations should also continuously look out for ideas and solutions that have been developed in other firms or industries.

Third, the concept of segments must be augmented to consider the psychological mindset of the customer at the time of the encounter. When bringing a car to be repaired, the customer is likely to be greatly agitated, and hence, the service provider should be trained to recognize this and react in ways that not only suggest empathy but that develop trust as well. Interestingly enough, the use of psychological engineering can yield major benefits by better understanding the largest demographic in much of the United States—senior citizens. Senior citizens, or the "gray market" as it is sometimes called, create particular challenges for technologically based encounters such as call centers. A pairing of the advantages of call centers contrasted with the characteristics of the gray market is given in the sidebar "Call Centers and Gray Markets."

Call Centers and Gray Markets

Call Center Characteristics	Characteristics of Gray Market Members
Advantages • No physical presence is required • Could be used any time and any day of the year • Could be used in direct sales • Respond to needs for information • Solve customers' problems and complaints in a short time • Automate process	• Require strong need for social interactions • Need for personal touch • Tend to be loyal to products and services • Physical limitations (mobility and hearing problems) • Need for easy use and access/convenience • Need time to process information • Have a lot of free time • Have technology aversion • Have difficulties in learning new tasks
Disadvantages • Long waiting time • Demoralized call center representatives (performance is based on the number and not on the quality of the answer provided)	• Detest being rushed

Source: Vassiliki Grougiou and Alan Wilson, "Financial Service Call Centres: Problems Encountered by the Grey Market," *Journal of Financial Services Marketing,* 7 (4), 2003, p. 362.

PROJECT EXAMPLES

Below we describe two assignments that illustrate how we incorporated the ETCs into process improvement projects. One of these projects included employees trained in Six Sigma and lean operations.

Project 1: Improving the Experience of Online Computer Purchases

Business Problem. A major online computer retailer was experiencing erosion in margins because of inbound phone calls inquiring about the status of pending orders. The firm had not yet implemented an order tracking system. Today it has an order tracking system that addresses many of the ETCs-related concerns.

Organization of the Project. A project team consisting of members from marketing, sales, call centers, and data analytics was led by a senior manager. The inbound phone calls were analyzed to determine the characteristics of customers who were calling. A significant percentage of the calls were attributed to first-time buyers and older buyers (over 45 years of age) who were concerned because they had no prior experience purchasing a high-ticket item on the web using a credit card. The transactions were then analyzed for psychological factors that influenced customer behavior.

Analysis of Emotions, Trust, and Control. Figure 8.1 is a flowchart that illustrates the information is linked in order to enhance perceptions of control and trust during the purchase process. The chart also shows the types of emotions customers may experience.

Solutions. Based on Figure 8.1, a set of recommendations was developed. The web pages were modified to incorporate information such as number of orders successfully delivered each month to demonstrate competence, security of the financial transactions was restated to enhance trust, and images of customers from a range of demographics were displayed to increase confidence in the customers' own actions. An e-mail was also sent confirming the transaction. The e-mail considered the possibility of postpurchase regret. In addition to reassuring customers about their choices, the e-mail explained the delivery process, when to expect the delivery, and what

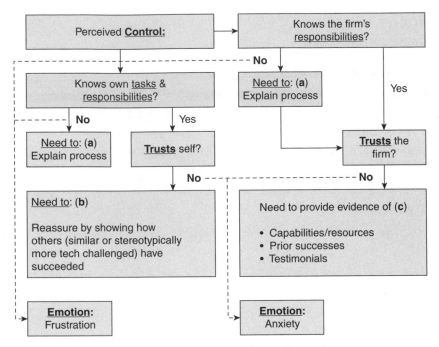

Figure 8.1 Analysis of control, trust, and emotions when customers are considering purchasing a computer on the web

customers needed to do on the day of the delivery, and it closed on a high note. The structure of the e-mail is shown in the sidebar "Confirmation E-mail."

Confirmation E-mail

An e-mail sent to customers immediately after the purchase had the following structure:

- **Emotions.** Reduce postpurchase regret: *"Congratulations."* "We are *confident* you will *enjoy* the product." "We take great *pride* in building your computer for you."

- **Trust.** "Last year alone we . . ." "We are the *leading* . . ." *"We were recognized* by . . . as the . . ."

- **Control.** "*The ball is now in our court.* In five days your order will be delivered to the address given below. In three days you will receive an e-mail with an exact delivery date."

- **Close on a positive note.** "We are *delighted* to have you as a member of the XYZ family."

Similar analysis was carried out for the full purchase cycle to identify when the firm should communicate and what the content of each communication should be based on ETCs considerations.

Project 2: Improving Interactions Between Nurses and Chronic Care Patients

Business Problem. Patients with chronic conditions, such as clinical obesity, chronic obstructive pulmonary disease, and acute diabetes, have to manage their health in order to maintain their quality of life and to avoid hospitalization. Patients and insurers benefit if patients stay healthy. Some insurance companies provide phone-based support to these patients. A large insurance company based in the Midwest wanted to improve the productivity and effectiveness of the interactions between nurses and patients. There were large discrepancies among the nurses in terms of their productivity and their ability to influence patients. The insurer wanted to structure the call content to make the calls shorter and more effective.

Organization of the Project. Nurses on the disease management team were randomly divided into two groups. One was the control group, and the other was the experimental group. Another team that included nursing supervisors, experts in lean operations, and change management supported the improvement project. On the first day everyone in the experimental group was introduced to the psychological constructs discussed in this book. Next the team identified different types of phone calls. For each of these calls the objectives and principal components or blocks in the conversation were identified. The teams then restructured the content and the sequence in which the conversations took place based on the following set of principles:

1. Get the bad news out early in the conversation.

2. Provide explanations and avoid jargon.

3. Take an interest in their socioemotional issues.

4. Segment out the good news and sprinkle it throughout the conversation.

5. Give patients choices.

6. Reinforce habits that are beneficial.

7. Finish on a strong note.

The project was implemented over eight weeks. Each day the nurses in the experimental group would huddle to discuss the new protocols. The calls by nurses in the experimental group were reviewed to see if the nurses adhered to the revised protocol.

The patients were surveyed on the following measures: satisfaction with the call, satisfaction with the nurse, belief in the nurse's willingness to help, motivation to change behaviors, belief in program's impact on health, willingness to recommend the program to others, and satisfaction with the insurer. The scores for the experimental group were significantly higher than those for the control group on all but three measures—satisfaction with the insurer, satisfaction with the nurse, and willingness to recommend. Satisfaction with the nurse and willingness to recommend for both groups were very high.

THINK IN TERMS OF THREE Ts AND FOUR Ps

At the beginning of this book we pointed out that the customers' experience can be parsed into three Ts: task, treatment, and tangibles. To deliver the experience, the firm has to develop what incorporates the four Ps: a set of service products, design processes, the right people, and the appropriate physical assets or environment. In the digital world, the physical environment is the web or graphic interface.

We know that quality and productivity of manufacturing systems advanced tremendously when craftsmanship was replaced by standardized production processes. The focus of this book is on processes. We identify approaches for embedding greater psychological savvy into systems and processes. We contend that this approach enables firms to deliver better experiences on a more consistent basis and reduces the burden of emotional labor.

We do not, however, wish to overstate our point. Developing a great experience requires that all four Ps are properly chosen. Swarovski's Crystal World is enchanting because of the sculptures and buildings. Web interactions with Fidelity are moderated by the aesthetics of the web page. If the nurses in the disease management program lack skills or are disgruntled, no amount of process redesign will improve the patient experience.

ETCs FOR EMPLOYEES

Show-off jobs. Throughout this book we take the perspective of the customer, but interestingly all the concepts can apply to employees as well. Certainly for restaurant servers there are high points that they enjoy in their jobs, for example, performing a task seamlessly, conveying good news, having customers know them by name, interacting with their favorite customers, being empowered to make important decisions, and being complimented for their performance by the customer. Along these lines, we have identified jobs that allow employees to show off their skills. The classic example is the hibachi chef at Benihana Japanese restaurants who puts on a show that demonstrates his skills with carving knives. What makes this particularly interesting is that it pulls the job from its traditional offstage location, a kitchen, and moves it onstage and in fact creates the unique niche for the restaurant. Other show-off jobs include docents at art galleries and museums, baristas at Starbucks, pizza makers, bartenders, the last guy at the carwash who makes a show out of polishing the car the last two minutes before the customer is hailed to pick up the car, and the glassblower in Venice who exaggerates his movements to emphasize his unique skills. In addition to their positive impact on the workers' morale, most show-off jobs have an obvious positive impact on sales. Some are to impress commercial buyers by presenting the skill and craftsmanship that go into a physical product. One pie manufacturer takes buyers from supermarkets to observe the skill and dexterity of the meringue "fluffers" on its lemon meringue and chocolate meringue pie production line. Most service jobs cannot be show-off jobs all the time, but there can be show-off opportunities at different stages of the service. For example, after a customer has signed the papers to buy a new Lexus, when the shiny new car is brought around after final detailing, the salesperson presents the key to the car wearing a white smock and gloves.

Service Recovery. Another major area where employees have a critical role to play in applying ETCs is in executing recovery actions to deal with service failures. In the attribution chapter we pointed out broad strategies for dealing with things that go wrong: let the punishment fit the crime, provide explanations, and so on. But service recovery is still an art under pressure, so we conclude with the following example of a recovery "artist" at work. See the sidebar titled "The Story of Harry."

The Story of Harry

While eating in the basement of a rustic Mexican restaurant in Boston, one of the authors and his wife observed a mouse run out from behind a stack of Cart Blanca beer cartons, nibble something, and scurry back along a wall baseboard. It so happened that one of the ovens was out that night, and though we had been informed of a likely delay for our meal, the manager came over to us and offered us a free dessert to make amends. We told him that it wasn't necessary and mentioned that we had just seen a mouse! His response: "A mouse: Oh, you mean Harry. Everybody knows Harry. And you know what the good news is? Mice and rats don't coexist." He then walked away, leaving us to appreciate the benefits of being under Harry's protection against the dreaded rats that roam the streets of Boston. Moral: A quick thinking manager reframed visible evidence of vermin infestation into a special positive feature of the service!

ENDNOTES

CHAPTER 1

1. Scott C. Beardsley, James M. Manyika, and Roger P. Roberts, "The Next Revolution in Interactions," *McKinsey Quarterly*, November 2005, 63–75.
2. See J. H. Fleming, et al., "Manage Your Human Sigma," *Harvard Business Review*, July–August 2005, 2–10.

CHAPTER 2

1. Joseph LeDoux, *The Emotional Brain* (New York: Touchstone, 1996).
2. Jonathan Barsky and Lenny Nash, "Employee Satisfaction Tied to Emotions, Company Beliefs," *Hotel and Motel Management*, Hotel/Motel.com, November 15, 2004.
3. Kevin Keller, *Strategic Brand Management*, 3rd ed. (Englewood Cliffs, NJ: Prentice Hall, 2008).
4. S. Das, C. Ellis, and C. Stenger, "Managing Tomorrow's Brands: Moving from Measurement Toward an Integrated System of Brand Equity," *Journal of Brand Management* 17, 2009, 26–38.
5. A. R. Hochschild, *The Managed Heart: Commercialization of Human Feeling*, 2nd ed. (Berkeley: University of California Press, 2003).
6. Robert Plutchik, "The Nature of Emotions," *American Scientist*, July/August 2001, 344–350.
7. Cam Tucker, "L.A. Kings Twitter Tweet Sends Canucks Fans' Fur Flying," *The Vancouver Sun*, staff blogs, April 12, 2012, retrieved December 9, 2012, http://blogs.vancouversun.com/2012/04/12/l-a-kings-twitter-tweet-sends-canucks-fans-fir-flying/.

CHAPTER 3

1. Uwe Dulleck and Rudolf Kerschamber, "On Doctors, Mechanics, and Computer Specialists: The Economics of Credence Goods," *Journal of Economic Literature* 44, March 2006, 5–42.
2. Kevin Keller, *Strategic Brand Management*, 3rd ed. (Englewood Cliffs, NJ: Prentice Hall, 2008).

3. Florian Stahl, Mark Heitmann, Donald R. Lehmann, and Scott A. Neslin, "The Impact of Brand Equity on Customer Acquisition, Retention, and Profit Margin," *Journal of Marketing* 76, July 2012, 44–63.

4. V. S. Folkes and V. M. Patrick, "The Positivity Effect in Perceptions of Services: Seen One, Seen Them All?" *Journal of Consumer Research, Inc.* 30, June 2003, 125–137.

5. Kettie Hetter, "How Would You Fix American Airlines," CNN Travel, October 5, 2012, http://www.cnn.com/2012/10/05/travel/american-airlines-turnaround-ideas/index.html.

6. Key Tourism Statistics, New Zealand Ministry of Business, Innovation & Employment, March 13, 2013, http://www.med.govt.nz/sectors-industries/tourism/pdf-docs-library/key-tourism-statistics/key-tourism-statistics.pdf.

7. Stephen Mihm, "Dr. Doom," *New York Times Magazine*, August 15, 2008, http://www.nytimes.com/2008/08/17/magazine/17pessimist-t.html?pagewanted=all&_r=0).

8. C. W. Hart, J. L. Heskett, and W. E. Sasser, Jr., "The Profitable Art of Service Recovery," *Harvard Business Review* 68 (4), 1990, 148–156.

9. G. V. Johar, M. M. Birk, and S. A. Einwiller, "How to Save Your Brand in the Face of a Crisis," *Sloan Management Review* 51 (4), summer 2010, 57–64.

10. E. Borgida and R. E. Nesbett, "The Differential Impact of Concrete Versus Abstract Information on Decisions," *Journal of Applied Social Psychology* 7 (3), 1977, 258–271.

11. B. Shiv, Z. Carmon, and D. Ariely, "Placebo Effects of Marketing Actions: Consumers May Get What They Pay For. *Journal of Marketing Research* 42, November 2005, 383–393.

12. N. H. Anderson, "Likableness Ratings of 555 Personality Trait Words," *Journal of Personality and Social Psychology* 9 (3), 1968, 272–279.

13. S. Dasu and R. Chase, "Redesign of Nurse Interactions with Chronically Ill Patients Based on Behavioral Science Principles: An Exploratory Field Study," USC Note, 2008.

14. B. E. Kahn and J. Baron, "An Exploratory Study of Choice Rules Favored for High-Stakes Decisions," *Journal of Consumer Psychology* 4 (4), 1995, 305–328.

15. Shakaib U. Rehman, Paul J. Nietert, Dennis W. Cope, and Anne Osborne Kilpatrick, "What to Wear Today? Effect of Doctor's Attire on the Trust and Confidence of Patients," *The American Journal of Medicine* 118, 2005, 1279–1286.

16. D. D. Kim, Y. I. Song, S. B. Braynov, and H. R. Rao, "A Multidimensional Trust Formation Model in B-to-C e-Commerce: A Conceptual Framework and Content Analyses of Academia/Practitioner Perspectives," *Decision Support Systems* 40, 2005, 143–165.

17. M. J. Bitner, "Evaluating the Service Encounter: Effects of Physical Surroundings and Employee Responses," *Journal of Marketing* 54, 1990, 69–82.

18. C. W. Hart, J. L. Heskett, and W. E. Sasser, "The Profitable Art of Service Recovery," *Harvard Business Review* 68, 1990, 148–156.

19. S. Dellande, M. C. Gilly, and J. L. Graham, "Gaining Compliance and Losing Weight: The Role of the Service Provider in Health Care," *Journal of Marketing* 68 (3), July 2004, 78–91.

20. S. Dasu and J. Rao, "A Dynamic Process Model of Dissatisfaction for Unfavorable, Non-routine Service Encounters," *Production and Operations Management* 3, fall 1999, 283–300.

21. I. Geyskens, J. Steenkamp, L. Scheer, and N. Kumar, "The Effects of Trust and Interdependence on Relationship Commitment: A Trans-Atlantic Study," *International Journal of Research in Marketing* 13, October 1996, 303–317.

CHAPTER 4

1. R. T. Mills and D. S. Krantz, "Information, Choice, and Reaction to Stress: A Field Experiment in Blood Banks with Laboratory Analogue," *Journal of Personality and Social Psychology*, April 1979, 608–620.

2. John E. G. Bateson, *Managing Services Marketing* (New York: Dryden HBJ, 1991), 97–98.

3. Elias H. Porter, "The Parable of the Spindle," *Harvard Business Review* 40 (3), 1962, 58–66.

4. Shouldice Hospital, Harvard Business Press Case # 805002-ENG-PDF, 2005.

5. Stephanie Dellande and Mary C. Gilly, "Gaining Customer Compliance in Services," in T. A. Swartz, D. E. Bowen, and S. W. Brown, eds., *Advances in Services Marketing and Management*, vol. 7 (New York: Jai Press, 1998), 265–292.

6. Jaime S. King, Mark H. Eckman, and Benjamin W. Moulton, "The Potential of Shared Decision Making to Reduce Health Disparities," *Journal of Law, Medicine, & Ethics* 39, spring 2011, 30–33.

7. Tiffany B. White, Gail A. Taylor, and Stephanie Dellande, "Extrinsic and Intrinsic Motivators of Customer Participation in Compliance Dependent Services," *International Business and Economics Research Journal* 2 (11), November 2003, 101–104.

8. Barry Schwartz, *The Paradox of Choice* (New York: Harper Collins, 2004), 91.

9. Shlomo Benartzi and Richard H. Thaler, "Heuristics and Biases in Retirement Savings Behavior," *Journal of Economic Perspectives* 21 (3), summer 2007, 81–104.

10. J. Komaki, M. R. Blood, and D. Holder, "Fostering Friendliness in a Fast Food Franchise," *Journal of Organizational Behavior Management* 2 (3), 1980, 151–164. Reported in Fred Luthans and Tim R. V. Davis, "Applying Behavioral Management Techniques in Service Organizations" in D. Bowen, R. Chase, and T. Cummings, eds., *Service Management Effectiveness* (San Francisco: Josey Bass, 1990), 177–209.

11. Robert E. Kraut and Paul Resnick, *Building Successful Online Communities: Evidence-Based Social Design* (Cambridge, MA: MIT Press, 2011), 142.

12. Mary Jo Bitner, Bernard H. Booms, and Lois A. Mohr, "Critical Service Encounters: The Employee's Viewpoint, *The Journal of Marketing* 58 (4), October 1994, 95–106.

CHAPTER 5

1. Stephen Farber, "Savviest Filmmakers Put Last Things First," *Los Angeles Times*, August 27, 2001.

2. D. Kahneman, B. L. Fredrickson, C. A. Schreiber, and D. A. Redelmeier, "When More Pain Is Preferred to Less: Adding a Better End," *Psychological Science* 4, 1993, 401–405.

3. D. A. Redelmeier and Daniel Kahneman, "Patients' Memories of Painful Medical Treatments: Real-Time and Retrospective Evaluations of Two Minimally Invasive Procedures," *Pain* 66 (1), July 1996, 3–8.

4. S. Dasu, "Note on Recollections of Obstetric Patients," 2010 Working Paper, Marshall School of Business, USC.

5. Ruth Bolton, "A Dynamic Model of Duration of the Customer's Relationship with a Continuous Service Provider," *Marketing Science* 17 (1), 1998, 45–65.

CHAPTER 6

1. William J. Friedman, *About Time: Inventing the Fourth Dimension* (Cambridge, MA: MIT Press, 1990).

2. B. F. Skinner, *The Behavior of Organisms: An Experimental Analysis* (New York: Appleton-Century-Crofts, 1938).

3. R. A. Block, E. J. George, and M. A. Reed, "A Watched Pot Sometimes Boils: A Study of Duration Experience," *Acta Psychologica* 46, 1980, 81–94.

4. Robert J. Graham, "The Role of Perception in Consumer Research," *Journal of Consumer Research* 7 (4), 1981, 335–342.

5. Ibid., 338.

6. Joseph Blackburn, *Time-Based Competition: The Next Battleground in American Manufacturing* (New York: McGraw-Hill Professional Publishing, 1990).

7. George Stalk Jr. and Thomas M. Hout, *Competing Against Time: How Time-Based Competition Is Shaping Global Markets* (New York: Free Press, 1990).

8. In the United Kingdom, one of the authors experienced the law of the queue as built into the British culture. I was waiting alone at a desolate country bus stop when a farmer arrived shortly afterward. He formed a one-person queue behind me to ensure that order was being maintained, even though no other people were there and the bus that traveled that route always had unused seats.

9. Oualid Jouini, Zeynep Aksin, and Yves Dallery, "Call Centers with Delay Information: Models and Insights," *Manufacturing & Service Operations Management* 13 (4), 2011, 534–538.

10. Brad Cleveland and Julia Mayben, *Call Center Management on Fast Forward: Succeeding in Today's Dynamic Inbound Environment* (Annapolis, MD: Call Center Press, 2002), 15–16.

11. Rongrong Zhou and Dilip Soman, "Looking Back: Exploring the Psychology of Queuing and the Effect of the Number of People Behind," *Journal of Consumer Research,* 29 (4), 2003, pp. 517–530.

12. D. DiClemente and D. A. Hantula, "Time Sensitivity in Online Shopping: Extensions of the Foraging Model," *Psychology & Marketing* 20 (9), 2003, 785–809.

13. Stefan Thomke, "R&D Comes to Services: Bank of America's Pathbreaking Experiments," *Harvard Business Review* 81 (4), 2003, 70–83.

14. Richard Larson, USC industrial engineering seminar, fall 2003.

15. Stephen Nowlis, Naomi Mandel, and Deborah McCabe, "The Effect of a Delay Between Choice and Consumption on Consumption Enjoyment," *Journal of Consumer Research* 31 (3), December 2004, 502–510.

CHAPTER 7

1. Chun-Ju Hsiao and Esther Hing, "Use and Characteristics of Electronic Health Record Systems Among Office-Based Physician Practices: United States, 2001–2012," NCHS Data Brief, no. 111, December 2012.

2. D. J. Simons and C. H. Chabris, "Gorillas in Our Midst: Sustained Inattentional Blindness for Dynamic Events," *Perception* 28, 1059–1074.

3. J. W. Schooler and J. W. Tanaka, "Composites, Compromises, and CHARM: What Is the Evidence for Blend Memory Representations?" *Journal of Experimental Psychology* 120, March 1991, 96–100.

4. J. Groopman, *The Anatomy of Hope: How People Prevail in the Face of Illness* (New York: Random House, 2003).

5. William Payton, "Getting in the Zone & Other Weird Gambling Rituals," *The Prescription Gambling & Sports Information* online newsletter, February 21, 2001.

6. Allen Kachalia, et al., "Liability Claims and Costs Before and After Implementation of a Medical Error Disclosure Program," *Annals of Internal Medicine* 153, 2010, 213–221.

7. Alicia Gallegos, "Massachusetts Hospitals Launch Patient Apology Program," *American Medical News* online, May 21, 2012, amednews.com.

8. E. T. Anderson, G. V. Fitzsimons, and D. Simester, "Measuring the Cost of Stockouts," Sloan School of Management, working paper, 2006.

INDEX

AAA, 68–69, 79–80
Ability, effort vs., 183–184
Action, inaction vs., 182–183
Active listening, 75, 81–82
Allstate, 38
Altieri, Mike, 52
Amazon.com, 66, 74, 82, 84
American Airlines, 66, 69
Anticipation, 15–16, 162–164, 376
Anxieties, addressing, 24
　　(*See also* Emotionally intelligent
　　　processes)
Apologies, 190–191
Apple Stores, 4, 167
Appraisal theory, 32–36, 49
Areas, Agatha, 75
Arizona Diamondbacks, 53–54,
　　85, 97, 154
Assessment:
　　and beginning of encounter,
　　　122–123
　　of dependent encounters, 127
　　factors influencing, 119
　　impact of highs and lows on,
　　　122
　　and peak and end rule,
　　　119–121, 123
　　of trustworthiness, 79–87
Assurance, 75
Attribution, 169–192
　　and ability vs. effort, 183–184
　　and action vs. inaction, 182–183
　　and assignment of
　　　responsibility, 179–182
　　channeling, 184–191
　　and discernment of cause,
　　　173–177
　　as factor in perceptions, 8–9,
　　　18–19
　　and memory tricks, 177–179
　　principles for managing,
　　　191–192

and recognition of success or
　　failure, 172–173
and subjective perceptions,
　　170–172
Automation, 20

Bank of America, 160
Barger, Jason, 23
Behavioral control, 90
Behavioral management, 112–113
Behavioral research, 4–5
Behaviors:
　　as cause of emotions, 26
　　determinants of, 19
　　that show interest, 74–75
Benartzi, Shlomo, 98–99
Benihana restaurants, 207
Berra, Yogi, 169
Bettis, Jerome, 43
Big data, 194
Biosense Webster, 17, 18
Bitner, Mary Jo, 115
Blackburn, Joseph, 151
Blind trust, 72–73
Block, Richard, 143
Body language, 76
Botti, Simona, 97–98
Brady, Tom, 63
Brand, 28–29, 37–38, 62–63
Bumrungrad International
　　Hospital, 109–110
Burnisom, Michele, 81–82
Bush, George W., 97

Caesars Entertainment, 42
Calculated trust, 72–73
"Cannot," "will not" vs., 85, 186
Capacity, 12
Cause and effect (*see* Attribution)
Causes:
　　discernment of, 173–177
　　of undesirable outcomes, 19

ABOUT THE AUTHORS

Sriram Dasu, associate professor at the Marshall School of Business, University of Southern California, has written numerous articles on operations management and continues to publish in leading academic and professional journals nationwide. His recent work focuses on employing psychological concepts to improve operations in a number of industries, including healthcare and financial services.

Richard B. Chase, Justin Dart Professor Emeritus, Marshall School of Business, University of Southern California, is the coauthor of *Operations and Supply Chain Management*, which sold over a million copies and is now in its thirteenth edition, having been translated into 12 languages. He is widely acknowledged as one of the founders of the service operations management field.